Shadows and Echoes

Shadows and Echoes

DOREEN FIOL

authorHOUSE®

AuthorHouse™ UK Ltd.
1663 Liberty Drive
Bloomington, IN 47403 USA
www.authorhouse.co.uk
Phone: 0800.197.4150

Published by AuthorHouse   10/01/2014

ISBN: 978-1-4969-9242-0 (sc)
ISBN: 978-1-4969-9243-7 (e)

Any people depicted in stock imagery provided by Thinkstock are models,
and such images are being used for illustrative purposes only.
Certain stock imagery © Thinkstock.

This collection of glimpses into the past is dedicated to
my husband, Pepe, to our lovely daughters,
Sarah, Victoria, Claire,
Caroline, Virginia and Sophia,
and through them to those who follow.
And also
to the memory of their dearly-loved
brother, Jonathan and our first
little one, Marcus – wherever they may be.

Long-fingered shadows,
Echoes of silent voices
Reach out from the past.

DBF

FOREWORD

'Memory Lane.'

That's a phrase I have heard and still hear. Often. What do we mean by it? Taking a stroll down 'memory lane' immediately evokes feelings of nostalgia, of the long-ago, of what used to be. I see it as a winding path full of long shadows and distant echoes. Where does it lead? And if I, as so many elderly people do, take that journey back along the years, what will I discover in those shadows, and whose voices will I hear in the echoes?

I find myself thinking a lot about memory lately. What is it? Why is it? When I die, as I must soon enough, will all my memories die with me? All those thoughts, all those feelings, all those journeys, a kaleidoscope of events, people, actions, decisions, anxieties, magic moments – will they all cease to exist when I go? And does it matter? And if it doesn't matter, why the wanderings in the dark, why the falls into the abyss? And why the view from the mountain top?

Suddenly I feel the need to write some of them down, to tell my story. No, not all of it. Not an autobiography. My life is not special enough – or maybe too special – for that. I have lived it and that is enough. The people I love and who love me already know most of it, have shared in it and together we make the whole. But parts of my story live only in my memory and if for no other reason I would like my children to know me before they knew me, before I became who I am today: when I was still a child, often lost in a somewhat alien world. Some of the memories have already been written about, have crept into my children's books and short stories and I'm sure have had a profound effect on me.

Often from this distance things look vague, blurry but occasionally something pops up that is bright as sunshine on water, clear as a child's smile. And sounds, now indistinct, may become clearer as I move nearer to their source.

Should I try to remember sequentially, chronologically, or would it be better to just drift along in the country of the past, meander, see what turns up? Or maybe it is like looking for beads in a broken necklace. Some are there, on the surface: glistening, attracting attention, easily recovered. Others have rolled away, become hidden, under furniture, in folds of cloth, down cracks in floorboards, in long grass, down drains, lurking in unseen, inaccessible places. Maybe some can be found after much probing and searching and shaking, others perhaps can be glimpsed but never retrieved. Only the space holding them remains to say that they ever were. And how to thread those that are retrieved? Can they ever be reassembled to make a whole close to the original? Not if their story is to be as true as possible. The placing, the focus, the grading, the lustre of the beads would have changed. Perhaps important ones, even valuable ones, from the original necklace would be missing, vaguely remembered but impossible to replace or recreate.

So I must try to remember as it was. Not coloured by hindsight. Not changed, however slightly, by each remembering. A difficult task. But is it possible?

I have often thought about the nature of memory. Without memory, do we exist? It is as though we are who we are through our memories and our place in other peoples' memories. It is there we recognise ourselves, identify ourselves, willingly or unwillingly. It is down memory lane that our emotions play – and sometimes play havoc. Long shadows and echoes that reach us even today. Some of the shadows are virtually impenetrable, some of the echoes silenced. Should I go there, perhaps into places I did not want to be and have no wish to go back to now? Would my journey into my childhood by complete – or honest – without travelling, once again, through those dark areas? How easy, how pleasant, to just reveal the bright, sunny days. How false.

Others have spoken of an idyllic childhood and I wonder what they mean by it. I think many, perhaps most, children suffer, whatever their situation. Even the loved, cherished and well-fed child has fears. Fear of the dark; the monster under the bed; strangers. Then, out of babyhood, there is fear of failure; of disappointment; of disapproval; of anger.

And what unspoken fears the adolescent suffers! And that suffering, real or imagined, either enriches them and helps them to grow or damages them irrevocably, limiting and distorting that growth.

Hindsight can brighten or darken the past but the reality with all its complexities is still there, somewhere.

Many of these early memories have come to me unbidden, without any prodding or poking: always there, part of the fabric of my childhood. Others, I suspect, will not be so easy to retrieve. Until I started this journey into the past I would have said I had a very good memory but now I find I am severely challenged. Do I actually remember that or have I heard it so many times that it has become as mine? Was it really like that or has time and distance enhanced, embellished or distorted it? How can we know? Can we know?

Despite all these unanswerable questions I shall start my journey and be ready to face up to whatever revelations may present themselves when I start poking around in the undergrowth, and shuffle my feet in the fallen leaves.

* * *

BEFORE THE WAR

Before I started school my day to day fears were simple. Dad in a temper rowing with Mum, Pamie and I keeping out of the way; cowering under the bedclothes hoping not to be noticed; keeping very quiet when the rent man knocked pretending not to be in; afraid of the hiss the gas mantle made when Mum lit it; afraid the gas could not be lit because we had not been able to save a shilling to put in the meter. That meant no light, no cooking or cups of tea. But these fears were soon dealt with. Dad would 'sleep it off' and be fine when he woke up, ruffling our hair, joking, telling us to be good for Mum. The money would somehow be scraped together and we would catch up on the rent; and eventually, one day in the future, there was the promise of electric light. People we knew who already had electricity paid their bill by the quarter. Three months, Mum and Dad said, would give us time to save up, putting more in the cocoa tin in good times and less when it was hard to scrape by.

I remember feeling afraid standing at the top of the long, long flight of stairs leading up to our two rooms at the top of the house in Clarendon Road near Granddad Goody's shoe-repair shop. I was told I fell down them once and was caught by the gas man. I have no memory of the fall but I do remember being carried upstairs by someone, my cheek against rough cloth. I have patchy memories of a cot, painted red standing in the corner of the room, me sitting on Mum's lap in an old chair beside it and on the landing, a gas-stove with a gas lighter hanging down attached to it which I was told not to play with. I remember the Hairdresser's shop on the corner and an Italian girl called Paola who worked there. I remember the workmen digging up the road and leaving the hole with broad planks across. I do not remember walking on to the planks but have a very vivid memory of looking up and seeing feet, lower legs and hands around the edge of the hole, and my Dad, very angry, pulling me out. I remember the sting of the slap on the back of my legs.

Sometime around this time I was sent away for a while. To where? Why? I have a name, Ashton Clinton, a place I have since found out is a place in Tring, Buckinghamshire. I think it was some sort of convalescent home, but what I was doing there I don't know. I think I was sent there either because I had been ill or because Mum was ill or maybe it was when she had Pam. Nobody told me and I never thought to ask. I remember an older girl in a yellow dress there, Hilda, who was my friend. She would push me on the swing, brush my hair and take me to the chickens to collect the eggs. The feel of those smooth, warm eggs, the smell of the hay and Hilda's yellow dress are my clearest memories of this time, just before I started school.

School started off badly for me. I recall feeling excited and nervous as my mother and I, with Pam in the pushchair, walked through the playground of St Francis Elementary School. A lady came out of the grey building and rang a large bell. The children milling about the playground lined up in rows facing her, all except for a handful waiting, like me, with their mothers along the wall. 'All the new ones line up here' she called, indicating an area to her right. Mum loosened my hand holding tightly to the pushchair and pushed me firmly towards the new line being formed. Some of the children were crying. 'Mummy will come and fetch you later, Dor,' my Mum said, and turned away towards the school entrance. I have a recollection of thinking she was going to cry. I would not cry.

Memories of that first class, when I was four and a half years old, have stayed with me. The brown desk, shared with a girl called Elsie who scratched a mark on the bench-seat to make sure I did not come over to her half. The rim-blackened hole in the desk for the porcelain ink-well kept filled with blue-black ink in the higher classes, we little ones were only allowed pencils and crayons. The brown covered Beacon reader. And especially the teacher, Miss Earsden.

Miss Earsden wore a built-up shoe and had a limp. She wore heavy glasses and had her hair up in a grey bun. She was also, I think, the unkindest person I ever met throughout my schooldays. At least that's how she appeared to me then, and, looking back, still does now. We soon learned that Miss Earsden did not like a child to appear to be too bright or interested. If your hand went up too quickly to answer a question she would deliberately pass you over to call on some poor child who she would deride for stumbling and stuttering, at the same time making remarks about 'show-offs' always wanting attention. If you were interested and actually asked questions you would be mocked, made to feel silly for asking. Her abilities for mocking a child into submission were powerful indeed. I fell victim to her talents very early on.

The Alphabet, upper and lower case, was written on the blackboard. We were to copy it into our exercise books then learn it by heart. I was caught staring out of the window, watching clouds.

'Oh, little Doreen, knows her Alphabet already, does she?'
'Yes, Miss.' I did. Mum had taught me.

A sniff, a pronounced 'tkt, tkt' then 'So little Doreen doesn't need to learn to read. Perhaps she can read already.' The class laughed nervously, sensing blood.

'Yes Miss, a bit.' I could, with difficulty, pick out quite a few words. She grabbed a book from the shelf behind her, opened it randomly and shoved it towards me. 'Read that,' she commanded, obviously angry. I didn't know what I had done wrong. I looked down at the book placed in my hands, hesitating. The picture on the left-hand side was familiar. It was a coloured illustration of Alice with the White Rabbit. I knew this book. My Auntie Rose had it and always regretted she hadn't got a little girl to read it to. Her only child, Lionel, was like his father, she said, only interested in what he could eat and drink and pigeons.

Miss Earsden was losing whatever vestige of patience she had left. She grabbed my upper arms and gave me a shake, making me almost drop the book. 'Read!'

I wanted to cry and I wanted a wee. *Please don't let me wet my knickers – not in front of the whole class – and her.* But whatever happened I would not cry. I started to read.

'D-own, down, down. W-oul-d – wowld- oh, *would* the f-all ne-ver come to an end?' She snatched the book, Alice's Adventures in Wonderland away from me.

'You're remembering it. You've had it read to you.' That was probably partly true but I had recognised the words and with my forefinger in place sounded them out. I spent the rest of the afternoon standing in the corner: my punishment for showing off. It was many years before I, a child who would read anything from bus tickets to weather reports, could pick up Lewis Carroll's delightful tale again. And it would be a very long time before I volunteered anything in front of a class again.

Mum knew I was unhappy at school and tried to ask questions. Looking back I think she thought I was being picked on by the other kids, particularly the boys. Mum did not like boys. But I was not being bullied by other children, at least no more than is usual for children playing and scrapping together. I don't think it occurred to Mum that my tormentor could be a teacher. I was thankful when, soon after, we moved and I could change schools. Later, in my next school in St Charles Square, and in my Grammar School, I enjoyed learning and would do all the written work to the best of my ability but I rarely was first to put my hand up. I never did like drawing attention to myself. I never felt comfortable in school. An interested and quite diligent student but always with that feeling of alienation, of not quite belonging. The fact that I was what was known as 'stocky' and had bad feet, making walking and running difficult, may have contributed to that. Playground games mostly involved running, skipping, jumping, playing hop-scotch: games from which I was often excluded, or excluded myself. I was too slow. But I was good at marbles, often being chosen to join and even lead small teams of boys in a corner out of the way of the children racing around in their more active pursuits. Consequently I played more with the boys than the girls and changed my place in class to sit beside a boy called Michael instead of the bossy Elsie. In my next school my best friend was also a boy, David, who remained my friend for many years, until we each met our respective life-partners.

Until I was eight years old my life was that of any other child reared in poverty in the back streets of West London. How to explain to today's children life before television, computers, mobile phones, electronic games? Our games were played in the streets. The lamp-lighter coming along at dusk to light the gas mantles and chase us home. Unless it was raining heavily playing indoors was not allowed. When we did it was board games or cards, Snakes-and-Ladders, Ludo, Snap, Noughts and Crosses, Hangman, colouring-in, using wax crayons, not paints. As we got older Draughts or Rummy joined the repertoire. Mostly, in out-of-school hours we ranged free. In the school holidays we were chased out after breakfast – a slice of dripping or margarine toast or, occasionally, a bowl of porridge or bread and milk – and told not to come back until teatime but to be sure to be back as soon as it was getting dark. If we were lucky we would be given a hunk of bread and dripping in a brown paper bag. Sometimes the bag was a blue one which meant it had contained the week's supply of sugar. The sugar combined with a liberal sprinkle of salt gave the bread and dripping doorsteps a well-remembered, distinctive flavour.

There was a lot of street life: horses and carts making deliveries, kids playing, women scrubbing doorsteps. Not just women, children too. I would often carry a bucket of water, cloth, scouring brush and a slab of hearthstone to clean long flights of front steps to the smart houses a few minutes and a whole world away. My little sister Pamela would help me, carrying the rough piece of grey hearthstone in her tiny hands and rubbing it vigorously on the wetted stone steps as I scrubbed. The pennies earned would be taken home to Mum. There was no sense of hardship, just pride in being able to make a contribution. We ran errands for people too, and helped carry shopping and packages but mostly we just played. I played in the street with the other kids. It wasn't like school where playtime was supervised, and to a large extent controlled by a teacher. In the street our games were many and varied and I could join in most of them as could little Pam and friends from other streets like David, and visiting cousins: 'What's the time, Mr. Wolf?' 'Pigeon Steps and Giant Strides', using the whole width of the road, dodging the horses and carts. Ball, marbles, skipping, whip and top, hoops, ropes on lampposts to twirl around in giddy circles, hop-scotch using a bit of blackboard chalk pinched from school, 'knocking-up-Ginger'. Ah, 'Knocking Up Ginger!' One of our favourites. How can you explain the thrill of creeping up front steps without being seen, tying black button-thread to a knocker, crossing the road without being spotted, doing the same to the opposite house, paying out the thread as we went, then, after a quick tweek, racing hell-for-leather down into the basement area of a nearby house to watch the unfolding drama. One of the doors would open thereby lifting the knocker of the opposite house. *Nobody there*. A look up and down the street. A 'tsk, tsk', a shake of the head and the door would close. In doing so the knocker of the first house would be lifted and banged down again and the whole pantomime would be repeated. Again and again, until it was realised by the now enraged occupants that they had been 'had'. Then the storming down steps, the search up and down the street, the near panic as we tried to smother our giggles and the real panic if we were spotted and had to run for our lives with shouts of 'just wait 'till I see your father'. 'I know where you live'. 'I'll tan the hide off yer ...' ringing in our ears.

Another game we loved was played at the Harrow Road end of Ladbroke Grove. A large black bridge spanned the railway running below. We would wait on one side of the road wondering who would be the first to see or hear the train. Sometimes a puff of smoke in the distance would announce its imminent arrival, sometimes it was the blast of the whistle. As it approached the bridge we would place ourselves between the girders so we would be caught and enveloped in the smoke. For a few moments we disappeared from view, then we would run across the road, dodging the traffic, mainly horses and carts, to catch more of the smoke on the other side. Dangerous – certainly. Stupid – undoubtedly. I'm sure it didn't do our lungs any good and for sure we would have had a few good hidings if our parents had known. But we were kids, and we loved it. We loved the excitement and the few moments when we were each totally alone in a grey-white cloud, but most of all I have a long, lingering, happy memory of the smell. There is nothing quite like the smell of the smoke from a steam train.

I remember the transient canal-boat children, 'Water-Gypies' we called them, who would come into my Elementary School before the War, when they were loading or unloading their barges on the Paddington branch of the Grand Union Canal. We were told, by teachers and nuns alike not to be unkind to them but not to become too friendly either, as they were sure our parents would not approve. Why? Because, we were told, they were *not like us.* What did that mean? And why did it mean we shouldn't mix with them? True, they were dressed differently, in a hotchpotch of colours and sizes, and their talk was rough – some of them 'swore like troopers' causing the nuns to turn away, crossing themselves. But that did not seem a good enough reason to me to shut them out. They interested me and the idea of living on a barge travelling up and down the waterway fascinated me. I became quite good friends with some of them. My Mum and Dad didn't mind although Dad didn't like the swearing. He used to swear under his breath, especially when in a temper but he would never allow us to do so and Mum never swore.

Children had freedom to wander in those days. At seven years old I could go 'up the Cut' after school as long as I took Pamie with me and didn't let her, or myself, fall in. Neither of us could swim. My new friends would come to our back street and sit on our front steps sharing a newspaper-wrapped pack of chips. They were impressed that we had two rooms and a scullery to live in as they all lived, father, mother, Auntie Vi, her 15 year-old son and the three younger children in one small cabin on the barge. The father and the boy I hardly ever saw as they were always working or walking the horse along the towpath. We were impressed by everything; the decorations on the barge, the beautifully decorated and ornamented cabin, the brightly-coloured kettle and teapot, the enamel mugs and the one-pot stews simmering on one burner. And of course we loved the patient old horse, Queenie. Queenie would give a little murmuring sound whenever we came near and nuzzle us in the hope of a titbit. She was big and very strong so we had to stay on the wall side of her in case she nudged us into the water. It was accepted by everybody, house dwellers and boat people alike, that intimate contact with the water of the canal was to be avoided under pain of catching every disease known to Man, and a few as yet undiscovered. The risk was probably not greatly over-exaggerated. 'The Cut', on the doorstep of large tenements, was used as a tip for all sorts of rubbish and waste. It was also the receptacle for many a bag of unwanted kittens and puppies and the last resting place of the occasional drunk. No, you would not want to swim in it.

When I returned from evacuation there were still longboats and barges on the canal carrying loads that would later be transported by rail and road. The Day Nursery where I started work was close to the Halfpenny Steps which led down to the canal and I would often walk along the bank in the hope of seeing my old friends again, but I never did.

Another memory has its place here. It is of an old lady called Miss Douglas. I have no real recollection of *her,* which is surprising as I know she has had a long-lasting effect on me. I presume she was old, as were all teachers and all the other kids' mothers, except mine. Not mine because she was so tiny – not much bigger than my eleven year old cousin. The lady in the sweetshop had a baby grandson so we knew she must be *very* old. She tried to make out she wasn't and coloured her hair to prove it, but we knew it was just pretend. Funny how I remember lots of things about the lady in the sweetshop; the coloured hair, how she peered at us over her glasses, the mole on her left cheek; a lady who never did anything special for me – and almost nothing of Miss Douglas, who did.

Miss Douglas lived near us in one of the poorest areas in London. It was scary going down the iron steps to her basement flat with the dark brown door. Sometimes Mum would lift me up so that I could give two sharp taps with the black knocker shaped like a lion's head and we would wait, listening for the muffled, slipper-clad footsteps and the scrape of the bolt. The door would open on to a narrow passage which was never lit and once the door was closed behind us we were enveloped in near-total darkness. Feeling our way past coats hanging on pegs, umbrellas, scarves, an oil-cloth shopping bag, and galoshes which I always managed to trip over, we followed the shadowy shape ahead until we reached a door, not quite shut. Behind the door was a heavy curtain which wrapped itself around me as I followed my mother into the room.

Despite the gloom – the curtains at the window were never fully opened – I can still see the room clearly. In the centre stood a large polished table covered with a green chenille cloth. On the table stood a tray set for tea, a squat brown teapot, a cut-glass mill jug, two cups and saucers, a child's British Empire mug and a wooden biscuit barrel with a porcelain lining and a chrome lid. An enormous bookcase filled with dark, important-looking books with gold lettering on the spines filled one wall. On the top shelf stood a faded sepia photograph in a silver frame. The couple, a young girl and a soldier, were standing close together and smiling. Along the adjoining wall stood a large sideboard covered in what my mother called knick-knacks. Photographs in a variety of frames and sizes, little boxes, tiny silver ones, a couple of wooden ones, one heart-shaped one containing who-knew-what, and, to one side, a silver tray holding a crystal decanter, two wine glasses and a single-stem crystal vase. Perhaps they were to remind Miss Douglas that she had known better days, my mother said.

An old rust-coloured chaise-longue with an embroidered velvet cushion ran the length of the bookcase facing the window with the almost-closed curtains. In the gap between the curtains there was a small table on which stood a large highly-polished brass pot containing an aspidistra whose long dark leaves, we were told, were washed with milk to make them shine. I would sit contentedly stroking the cushion, looking at the aspidistra, which seemed to have a face when you stared at it long enough and appeared to be my friend. The only other item in the crowded but tidy room was, in the far corner, a pedestal with a tall but empty birdcage. Drinking milk from the mug, being allowed to sort through the biscuits to find the unbroken ones – we only ever had broken biscuits at home when we had them at all – Miss Douglas' basement, so full of comfort and interest and questions that were hardly ever asked and never answered, was no longer a place to be feared.

I don't know how Mum knew Miss Douglas. My family was, as were most people around us, very poor. Miss Douglas, I think, was not poor. Poor was when you had no money left and no possessions left to sell or pawn. You could tell how things were with us by whether the clock (necessary in case Dad got work) was in its place on the mantelpiece and Dad's overcoat on its peg, or if there were just spaces, the pawn tickets kept safe in the Oxo tin until better days. Anything that could be permanently dispensed with had been sold long ago. Miss Douglas still had lots of possessions, always in the same place. Miss Douglas was, in our estimation, comfortably off.

For some reason none of us could understand Miss Douglas took a fancy to me. I was not sunny-natured, sweet or pretty as was my little sister. Everyone loved Pam. When not with other kids in the street I was quiet, serious, I would sit watching, often with a frown. 'A thinker' people said kindly, glad I wasn't theirs. 'Bit of a dreamer.'

I remember the day I knew Miss Douglas liked me. I was sitting on our front steps watching ants. Mum came along with her shopping-bag. It was heavy and she had to keep putting it down for a 'breather.' As I said, she was only a little dot.

'If you are a good girl Miss Douglas is taking you to the Pantomime on Saturday.' This was an almost unheard-of, barely believable outing; the sort of thing that only happened in books or to those living in the big houses in the other Kensington near Hyde Park, not our North Kensington which was just slums around the Gas Works and the canal.

That first theatre experience was amazing. There were a lot of children, a buzz of excitement and Miss Douglas bought me an ice-cream. The lights went down, the music started – and a world of dazzling richness exploded around me, swamped me, sucked me in, swallowed me up. Colour: Light: Excitement: Delight! Oh, the magic of it! The never-to-be-forgotten wonder!

It was dark when we came out and the lamp-lighter was lighting the street-lamps. They glowed yellowish, the gas pop-popping gently. When we reached our corner some children were still playing on the steps.

'Where you been?'

'Out.' Some things are too wonderful, too beautiful, too intense, to share.

Of course I outgrew the pantomime. It's theatre now, concerts, and most of all, opera. But I have never out-grown the sense of – no, the belief, in – magic.

Who was Miss Douglas? I wish I knew her story. I wonder if Mum knew it and if so, why she never told me, and why I never asked. Who were the people in the photographs? Why was she still *Miss* Douglas? Why two wine-glasses and did anyone ever buy her a flower for the single-stem vase? Was there ever a bird in the cage? A parrot perhaps, or a pair of love-birds? When, why and from where had she 'come down in the world?' I cannot even remember what she looked like, how she was dressed, whether or not she wore glasses. I cannot see her with my inner eye, cannot hear her voice nor remember anything she said or even if she smiled. A shadow lady. Yet I sense her substance still, feel her touch holding my hand and think of her still with gratitude and affection. She gave me a gift which is as priceless today as it was then, all those years ago. The ability to *know – for sure –* that somewhere, something beautiful is happening. And sometimes, I, too, may share in it.

I suppose life was hard for our parents but we were, if not unaware of it, untroubled by it. We made our own fun with very little input from the adults, unless we were in need of chastisement. Correction and punishment was usually physical. Children were treated quite roughly: smacked by teachers, mums and elder siblings, dragged by the hair or ear, the use of the ruler and the cane at school, spanked with a slipper. All quite normal. Only if a stick was used or we had had the taste of Dad's belt did we think it was worthy of more than a mention, then it was more in indignation and a sense of injustice than any question as to whether or not it should have happened. 'Spare the rod and spoil the child' was the order of the day. You would be considered a bad parent if your child didn't get 'a good walloping' now and again. Mum didn't smack us much, probably because she had very small hands and couldn't make much impression, but she could be quite terrifying chasing us with a broom. And she could be quite powerful with the threat used by mothers everywhere 'just you wait till your father gets home'. Waiting in anticipation and fear was not a nice state to be in and both Pam and I would be little angels for the rest of the day, hoping that Mum might relent and not report our misdoings. If Dad raised his hand, Pam would start to cry, but I was stubborn and would not cry, making the situation worse. I was always considered the most at fault, as I was the eldest. Whatever Pamie had done I shouldn't have let her do it. I thought that wasn't fair and would say so, bringing down more retribution on my head. Born to be a diplomat I wasn't.

Dad, despite his constant battle against the dreaded tuberculosis, did his best for us when he could. He was a hard-working man, well-respected among those who knew him and by other workers and his bosses whenever he had work. True, we were nervous of his short temper, but not nervous enough to stop me provoking him with my stubbornness. And there were the other times, like during storms or if Pam or I had a nightmare, when he would stay with us and reassure us and we knew that while he was there we were safe. Mum was a very tiny, fiercely proud, lively woman who stood four feet eight inches in her size twelve shoes and weighted, as her heaviest, six stone twelve pounds. Her one big complaint was that, because she had such tiny feet, she could only get shoes in children's styles. Later in life she had a pair of lasts made to her size and was able to order, to her great delight, proper grown-up shoes, made to measure. She was very pretty and took great pride in her appearance and that of her two daughters. However tired she was she would brush our hair nightly, putting mine into ringlets or 'finger curls' and Pam's into metal curlers covered with a hairnet. I would then brush Mum's hair and put the curlers in all around her head. Each of us, all the while, fine-tooth comb handy, would be on the look-out for nits or, horror of horrors, 'runners'. A Nurse – irreverently called 'Nitty Norah' – still attended the schools and the mortification of livestock being discovered in a child's head was indescribable. Some actually had their heads shaved and painted with Gentian Violet, the attention-claiming power of the bright purple, causing much more distress than ever the irritation from the infestation had done. From the day we went to school my Mum never risked it so we never had to suffer that shame.

She kept us clean too, which with no hot water was not an easy task. There was an old copper set in a concrete block in a corner of the scullery. We would light a fire in the gap under it and fill it with buckets of water from the tap. Quite a difficult task for such a diminutive lady, which I took over as soon as I was able. We would then give the clothes a good boil, popping in a 'blue bag' to help whiten the whites, and scrubbing dirt and stains on the rubbing-board with a hard brush and a square bar of Sunlight soap. The clothes had then to be left to cool a bit after the fire went out and transferred to the deep old Butler sink to be given several rinses in cold water and put through the mangle in the yard before being pegged out on to the washing line. How delighted we were whenever Dad had some work so we could pile all the dirty washing in an old calico pillow-case and take it on an old pushchair around Portobello Road to the Bag Wash, where it could be picked up later, washed and damp-dry, ready for ironing. The ironing was done with flat irons heated on the gas, the smell of damp clothing pervading the atmosphere for days. I liked ironing so usually volunteered for that, although Dad would do his own shirts. I remember Mum teaching me to spit on the iron to see if it was hot enough. It had to sizzle and the spit run off at just the right speed. Too fast, it was too hot and would scorch the clothes; too slow and it would just raise steam without removing the creases. She taught us other things that were important to her. Never to lean back on damp clothes drying on the backs of chairs or we'd get pneumonia; always to dry our hands thoroughly or we were asking for rheumatism; to remember to dry between our toes after our Friday night ritual in the old tin bath or we'd get foot-rot. These things worried her and I remember, many years later, as I was sitting beside her as she lay dying, caring for us was still on her mind. She was delirious, rambling 'Don't lean back on that wet towel, Dor, you'll catch your death.'

We hadn't got much, but what we had felt solid, unshakeable. We played we fought, we dreamed. And, ah, the expectation, the hope. Tomorrow was always going to be better.

Then came the War.

During the War

Some of my most powerful memories are war memories. The Second World War. The one that followed the 'War to End all Wars.' We'd been brought up on stories of that terrible time, of the trenches, the gassing, the hideous suffering, and everyone knew someone, now old, old, men, whatever their age, who had been there. That was never going to happen again. But it did. My Dad said that all we had learned from History was that it repeats itself.

I find I'm still inclined to divide events, people, happenings, into before the war, during the war and after the war.

I began by shambling around in the somewhat shady time before that significant era, seeing what I can remember – rediscover – of the child who, at just eight years old, was taken, along with what seemed hundreds of other children, to be transported by train from Paddington Station to 'the Country'. I have two very clear memories of that actual journey, both connected with guilt. The first was the certain knowledge that the War was all my fault and the other was the question which took some years of grown-up thinking to answer: Why were Mum and Dad, and my little sister Pam staying in London together, while I was being sent away? Until then

I had been Mum's little right-hand-girl, helping her look after little Pam, fetching and carrying, turning the washing airing on the clothes-horse in front of the stove, brushing her hair and helping her put her curlers in. She had often said she could not manage without me, told people what a good little girl I was. So why was I on this train being taken somewhere else? What had I done? I felt I must have done something very bad. These feelings, which grew as the train gathered speed and took me further and further away from everything I had ever known, stayed with me for a long time. A very old-fashioned, Catholic School background did nothing to help!

I thought it was going to be difficult remembering, trying to piece the fragments together, but recently illness gave me the opportunity to drift into less controlled areas of thinking and I found myself arriving effortlessly into half-remembered times.

I recall clearly the day the guilt was removed. I say 'removed' and not 'went away' because that was exactly what happened. It was removed in its entirety as with a surgeon's knife, leaving a clean, empty space. A space thereafter occupied frequently by little guilts – after all, all well-brought-up Catholic youngsters can find *some* – but never again has that space been so totally filled.

It had all started at the end of August 1939, a few days before War was declared. My mother had returned from a visit to the pawn-shop, her left hand bare, and in the passage stood a battered compressed cardboard suitcase with catches that clicked open and shut. The catches delighted my little sister and me until we were shouted at to leave them alone. Pam did so immediately, but I sneaked back several times to have another go. I had a feeling it was going to be my suitcase.

There was a package on the scullery table and I'd peeped in. It contained knickers, vests and liberty bodices – my size – a new flannel and towel, and a comb. In a separate brown paper bag there were two pairs of new white socks. I couldn't remember having new clothes before. Two old dresses had been lengthened, washed and ironed: the unfaded bit looking like a false hem and Mum had got me some leather shoes in Portobello Market that were not too badly scuffed and were only a bit too big. My coat was perfect. Last year it had been miles too big but was now just right. The case was packed, and then we waited. I didn't know what we were waiting for and nobody answered my tentative questions.

One morning during the waiting time Mum took me to the sweet-shop. This was a very rare occurrence. 'Don't tell little Pam' whispered my mother. 'George, keep Pamie in the kitchen when we come back,' she called as we reached the basement door.

The sweet-shop was familiar to me, mostly from the outside where I spent long minutes gazing in. Occasionally I had been inside, to spend an illicit farthing (picked up in the street) on two black-jacks. Once, having whitened a lady's doorstep with hearthstone (a job I did frequently to take pennies home) she gave me a penny extra. That day I stood in the shop, trying to choose, savouring every moment, until the shop-lady lost patience and said if I didn't hurry up she wouldn't serve me at all. At that I became very flustered and bought all black-jacks as I didn't know what the other things tasted like, except barley-sugars and aniseed balls which were in a jar on the top shelf and I thought she might be cross if I asked her to get them down. Anyway they were a penny each so I would only get one.

'Two sticks of Barley-sugar please' (one for me and one for Pam? But why weren't we to tell her?)

'You'll be off soon, then?' the shop-lady said, addressing me. I looked at my mother.

'Friday', she said.

'Looks certain then,' said the shop-lady, popping the two twisted, amber sticks into a paper bag.

'It still could blow over,' my mother answered, not believing it.

'Gotta keep our peckers up, for the sake of the children,' the shop-lady said cheerfully, smiling at me. ''Bye 'bye, dearie. Have a nice time in the country.'

So I was going to the country. I had a grandma, and cousins and aunties who lived in the country, where Dad came from. Tilbury, in Essex. I remembered Dad taking us there once when I was about five, to Uncle Denis's and Auntie Myrtle's wedding. We went on the train and walked the last part of the way along the railway track to their cottage at Lowe Street. Perhaps we were going there? I wasn't sure how I felt about that. I had been in big trouble there on account of my dislike of being 'dressed up', in what I saw as fussy clothes. As I was to be a bridesmaid I was dressed in a pale green, flowery organza dress with puff sleeves. This, along with green satin hair ribbons I could just about cope with, but it had *frills*. Several tiers of them encircling the skirt from waist to hem. The puff sleeves I could do nothing about, nor the buttons and bows down the front of the dress, but the frills I didn't have to tolerate. Sitting quietly in a corner while everyone got ready for the Church I found a loose thread and methodically unpicked and carefully rolled up each frill, being careful not to tear the fabric of the skirt as I pulled the last stitches away. The end result looked a bit like a petticoat or a nightie but it pleased me. Not so the adults. Needless to say I was not a bridesmaid that day, but was squashed between my parents in a pew at the back of the Church, kept respectably hidden so as not to be seen in the group photographs, and made very aware that I was not anybody's favourite child. Dad had been back since, but not the rest of us. I felt quite troubled at the thought of meeting them all again.

We left the shop, smiling and waving, feeling all serious inside, which puzzled me. I fixed my thoughts on the barley-sugar. There it was, two whole sticks of it. And at least one was for me: I was sure of that.

Back home we opened the suitcase and placed the sweets, wrapped in an extra piece of greaseproof paper, on top of the clothes.

'Now, you are not to touch them until you are on the train.' (Mummy and Daddy were not coming then?) 'Have one when the train starts and the other when you are about half-way – one of the grown-ups will tell you.' (so they were both for me – little Pam wasn't coming either).

'Where, Mummy? Where am I going? Why are you sending me away?'

'All the schoolchildren are being got out of London in case there's a war, love. If there is – and it still might not happen – it'll be over in a few weeks and you can come home again.'

'Can't you and Daddy and Pamie come too?'

'No, love. The school children are being evacuated with their teachers.'

What did evacuated mean? It was all very confusing and I was troubled.

On Friday my father took me to school. He had the suitcase in his left hand and held my hand in his right, his bad hand, the one with the lumps in it. Mummy cried as she waved from the top of the steps and Pam started to cry too, I think because Mum was crying.

The school hall was filled with children and suitcases and crying parents. A teacher was checking information against her list. She made out a label with my name and a number and an address I didn't know and tied it through my button-hole. I was given a box containing something heavy. 'Don't bang it and don't lose it – it's your gas-mask. Say goodbye to your father now.' All said with a tight smile and mock cheerfulness.

Daddy stood for a moment at the door and I thought that perhaps he would change his mind and not let me go, but some latecomers arrived and he had to move out of the doorway. I watched for a while in case he came back for me. But he didn't.

Time passed slowly. Someone went into the Headmistress's office to listen to the news on the wireless. Maybe they would come back and say there wasn't going to be a war and we could all go home. I'd give one barley sugar to Pamie and we'd sit on our front doorstep sucking it. It would last ages, even if we let the other kids in the street have a lick.

Perhaps I could just have a lick of one barley sugar now? After all, if we were really going away no-one would ever know, and if we weren't surely one little lick wouldn't notice once it dried. I'd give Pam the unlicked one.

I opened the case as if to check its contents and pulled out the packet. Turning towards the wall I surreptitiously licked. Nobody took any notice. Some of the children were already eating bread-and-dripping doorsteps or jam sandwiches. Of course, it didn't stop at one lick. The lovely, golden stick shortened, changed shape, becoming pointed at the top, the pointy bit beginning to bend over. No doubt now, it was half-gone. Might as well finish it. I looked at the other one, still unlicked in its wrapper. If we went home now, I would be found out anyway. Oh, well!

I finished the barley sugars – both of them. I looked towards the office door.

Suppose they came back and said there's not going to be a war after all? Oh, there must be a war – please – there *must* – just a little war – just enough for us to get to the country. Once there I would be expected to have eaten them. I can't go home without them in the suitcase. There MUST be a war – just a little war … please … *please.*

I remember feeling guilty, sitting biting my nails and watching the door, half dreading, half hoping that my Dad might come back to get me after all. I didn't relax until I was on the train. It was alright now. God could finish the war and we could go home.

Arriving at the little country town with trees in the streets and flowers growing in front gardens I felt happy and light. Mum was right; it would be lovely to stay here for a little holiday until they took us home again. We walked in a sort of straggly procession. A teacher talked beside me.

'I hope you've got a hairbrush,' she said, looking disapprovingly at my tousled mane.

'No, miss, I haven't never had a hairbrush of my own.' I said, remembering my 'aitches' and being careful not to say 'aint' which my mother said was common. 'But I got a comb. Me Mum had to keep the brush 'cos of little Pam,' I added conversationally. This was met with a blank stare and the teacher moved on down the line. Gradually the crocodile of children thinned out and shortened as, in ones and twos, children were handed over doorsteps to waiting strangers and checked off against the Billeting Officer's list.

The first couple who took me had a daughter, Ann. 'You must call me 'Mum', Ann's mother told me 'and this is 'Dad'. You can be the other little girl we've always wanted.' No, I couldn't. So I didn't call them anything. I knew I could never call her 'Mum'. My mum was at home, with my sister Pam, and my Dad. Home was a couple of rooms in a back-street London tenement, not here in this wide, tidy Dorchester street where families had a whole house to themselves, with paths and garden gates and trees in the street. The leaves, already beginning to fall, had been swept into tidy piles. Some days later when sent on an errand, I kicked angrily into the piles and as they scattered around me I remember experiencing a sudden sense of joy, I suppose exhilaration. To this day, if no-one is looking, I will still shuffle through fallen leaves and feel that pleasure. I had already registered the beauty of the late sunflowers and roses behind the garden gates but I suppose in my confused state I was not ready to let in anything to offset the bad feelings – until nature – and perhaps the resilience of childhood – did it for me. This first family didn't keep me long, just a couple of weeks, I think, then I was sent to another couple, Mr and Mrs Hare, in Monmouth Road, Dorchester, who already had four evacuees and allowed us to call them 'auntie' and 'uncle' which wasn't quite so bad. I stayed with this elderly couple, 'Uncle Jack and Auntie Nell', until I was transferred to the Midlands after my Scholarship. The 'Auntie Nell' bit was difficult, as my Mum's name was Nellie, so I generally stuck to 'Auntie'. They were quite good to us, feeding us well and not dealing with us too harshly when we misbehaved. They even took me back – not exactly with open arms – after I had run away. They, and my Headmistress, Miss Shepherd, told me how ungrateful I was and said I was 'a bit of a handful' but, surprisingly, I received no specific punishment.

Two days after our arrival – 3rd September 1939 – war had broken out. There were frequent News bulletins, listened to with hushed attention, which told of losses, planes shot down, ships sunk, men taken prisoners of war far from home, or worse, not coming home at all. And then there were the bombs. With the bombing of London, where my Mum, Dad and little sister were, I realized the enormity of what I'd done. My sense of guilt, which had nagged at me quietly from the first realization of what war really was, became overwhelming. The little girl, Maureen, who lived next door but one, came in one day with her mother. They were in tears and Mrs Varlow was 'all to pieces' as Auntie put it, because she said that three weeks previously she had seen her husband in what she thought was a dream go down with his ship. 'His last words were 'I'm sorry, Doll' she sobbed. And on this morning she had received the dreaded telegram telling her it was so. Had she had what my Mum would have called a premonition? Had that been a coincidental dream? Her husband was at sea, during wartime, and therefore in a very dangerous situation, so it would be reasonable to think so. I don't know. It all looked very genuine to me, and even looking back I can still hear the puzzlement in her voice as she questioned the meaning of that last message.

I became difficult after that. Remote, silent, intense, happier with animals than people. I would wander alone for hours 'communing with nature' as my Headmistress once said in my defence. In those days we did not have disturbed children who became teenagers with special needs, we had difficult, troublesome children who became juvenile delinquents. Fortunately, before the second stage had set in, my young mind had been relieved of its burden. The relief was enormous.

Solitary and unhappy, I had decided to run away. I would go home. I hung around the coach station for a while, hoping that maybe I could sneak on a bus unnoticed but soon realized I was attracting attention. I would have to walk to London.

Having been on the road for a couple of hours, on a hot summer's day and nearing Puddletown, I was tired, hungry and extremely thirsty. A man fell in step beside me. He offered me a drink and a sandwich and said we should sit in the shade. We entered a field and had been sitting by the hedge, out of sight of the road, I waiting for the promised refreshment, when he made the suggestion. I got to my feet, and, I think with dignity, walked away, climbing carefully over the gate so as not to show my knickers. He shouted after me 'you've run away. I'll tell on you.' I didn't look back, he did not follow. Only in later years did I realize what a lucky escape I had had. I kept to the sides of the fields after that, not wanting to be seen from the road in case he told the police.

Eventually I came to a travellers' camp. Gypsies! We had always been warned about Gypsies but I had met some of them when they came selling from door to door and I liked them. They usually had their children with them, keeping them close and not letting anyone pick on them. I liked that. Also, before the war, when visiting my father's family, my cousin Mary and I had known the Gypsies up on Chadwell Hill in Essex. We had played with them, gone conker-gathering with them and not had the same fear of them that people generally seemed to have. True, they were rough, quarrelling a lot – which they seemed to enjoy – swearing, shouting, the grown-ups threatening the children with all sorts of terrifying consequences if ever they got hold of them. But I don't remember a Gypsy child ever being hit. They were happy and cheeky, running off laughing, getting away with things we would never have dared even try.

I went towards them, keeping a wary eye on the horses, skirting the dogs tied to the wagons, setting them barking. Some boys threw sticks at me but their mother told them to stop it. She didn't ask my any of the questions grown-ups usually ask children, like how old are you, where are you going, what are you going to be when you grow up; she just said 'sit down, girlie', shooing a chicken out of the way beside her. It scuttled off to join other chickens (bantams I now know them to have been, looking back) under the wagon. I sat down, leaning against the wheel and she brought me some stew and some homemade lemonade without saying very much at all. One of the boys who had been throwing sticks gave me some chocolate and tried to make me have a puff of his cigarette. Several of the children were smoking, as were most of the adults. This didn't surprise me as Mum and Dad smoked and even little Pam had a drag on Mum's Woodbine occasionally. I never wanted to smoke, I don't know why, as almost everybody else I knew did. I ate the chocolate, then slept.

When I awoke a wireless was blaring from one of the caravans. They news was the usual thing: they had killed some of ours but we had killed a lot more of theirs. One lady was crying. From their talk afterwards I learned that Gypsies were hated and driven out just like the Jews. I didn't know much about Jews, except that Jesus and his mother were Jews and before marrying Dad, Mum had worked in service for Jews who were very good to her. They sounded like nice people to me and these Gypsies seemed nice too. I thought it was strange to belong to something that was hated just for being what it was. I told them I didn't understand that. The old lady, the boys' Gran I think, then said something I have never forgotten; I can still head her gravelly voice saying 'no-one of us can unnerstan' it, girlie. We on'y know what will 'appen will 'appen and their'm nuthin' none on us o'yous can do t'change it.' I told them about the barley sugar. How responsible I felt. How this terrible war was due to me asking God to cover for the naughtiness. Not so, they assured me. It had been 'in the air' a long time. Everyone had known it had to happen. 'No bitti child' was to blame,' the Gran assured me. Her own chavvies 'wus as bad as any' she said with obvious pride. They all agreed and laughed heartily, the old lady slapping her thighs and coughing, wiping away tears on her skirt. 'Por' li'l girlie! Twe'r'nt yor doin'.' They continued to laugh – and I laughed with them, although I remember I felt tearful too – and it was over. I knew 'chavvies' meant children. Mary and I, along with most of the kids in that part of Essex, had acquired quite a vocabulary of Romany words. Even today, you will still hear 'kushti' used to mean good or okay, 'bosh' meaning a load of rubbish, a 'rum cove' for a strange or odd fellow and 'chav' is in general use, but as a critical term for a certain type of youth. Then it just meant 'child', usually a Gypsy child. I don't know if they told the police I was there. And somehow it didn't matter.

I was sent back to London to be with my parents for a while. I expected to be in a lot of trouble, maybe even get a hiding with my Dad's belt, but to my surprise nobody said anything except 'Hello, love, we've just got time for a nice cup of tea before going down the shelter'.

I never told them about the barley sugar. Nor the man.

Going down the shelter meant a half-hour walk to Notting Hill Gate to sleep on the Tube Station platform, away from the bombs. Dad carried old grey blankets and a bag on his back with Tizer bottles filled with water, Mum carried bread and dripping sandwiches, a flannel and her inevitable handbag, Pam carried an enamel mug and I a tin bucket – the china po was too heavy and might get broken. I dreaded having to use the bucket in front of everybody and eventually wet myself and my patch of blanket. At five o'clock next morning I had to walk the long walk home with wet knickers.

There were jagged spaces where, only last night, houses had been. Not empty spaces, spaces willed with dust and smoke and activity as the rescue services got to work. Spaces framed by inside bedroom walls, a mirror on the wall of a non-existent bathroom, the head of a stairway, leading nowhere. We hurried past fire engines, ambulances, shocked people clutching mugs of tea. Heads down, trying not to see, we stumbled over debris and I tripped over a dead Airedale dog. I cried the rest of the way home, partly for the dog but partly, I think, with relief that I had not been instrumental in all this devastation. I know this is with hindsight, but I do remember a feeling, like I used to get when wandering about by myself, a sense of release, of freedom.

Every morning as soon as the 'All Clear' had sounded, we streamed out of the tube-station exits or shelters and made our way home. At that time there were few raids during the day so we children would wander the streets, watching rescues, being pushed aside, partly for our safety but as much to keep us out of the way, as we watched the fires and the buildings crumble and fall.

Some time later I was returned to Dorchester where I was still inclined to solitary wanderings but was otherwise very little trouble. I still couldn't understand why I was there and Pam, now at school, stayed at home. At one point Pam did come and stay with us, making us five evacuees in all: me, Pamie Glascock, Sylvia Glascock, Jane Dye and my Pam, and I thought at least we were together, but Pam went home again after a couple of weeks. I never knew why. At the end of the way the family 'Auntie Nellie and Uncle Jack' adopted Pamie Glascock – but not her sister Sylvia. Bewildering to children are the ways of adults!

Along with other ten and eleven year-olds I sat the Scholarship – which later became the eleven-plus – and a story of mine was entered into a competition – an Exhibition of Children's Literature. My Headmistress, Miss Shepherd, said I had won a place to a good Grammar school. A choice of two. Brompton Oratory and St Aloysious Convent. Both schools, based in London, had been evacuated. To accept a place I would have to go away to another place. No problem.

I had no attachment to anyone or anything. I was allowed – presuming parental guidance – to choose. My parents knew nothing about posh schools. You left school at fourteen and went to work to earn your bread. Anyway they weren't there to ask. We had no telephone – very few people had – and kept in touch by occasional letters that said nothing except to confirm our existence and state of well-being.

'Dear Mummy and Daddy,

I hope you are well. I am well and I hope little Pamie is well too. I got good marks in school today and got a sweet. They make me wear gloves to stop me biting my nails. They are tied on with string. I don't like them and everyone laughs at me. I hope you keep safe from the bombs. With love from Doreen xxx'

'Dear Doreen,

Thank you for your letter. Mummy and I are surprised to see you are staying at a different address. Pamie says why can't we come to see you. She doesn't understand Dorchester is a long way away. We tell her the War will soon be over, then you can come home. In the meantime be a good girl. I'm sending you a postal order for five shillings to buy some sweets. Love from Daddy, Mummy and Pamela xxx.'

Choosing a school when the time came posed no problem for me. Without consultation with anyone I opted for St Aloysious for one very good reason, and one reason only. The Oratory's uniform, which, in those days included knickers and socks, was navy-blue, the Convent's brown. Navy-blue meant navy-blue knickers, which we had always worn throughout Elementary school. Nothing in this world was going to get me into navy-blue knickers ever again. The brown won. I think my Headmistress, Miss Shepherd, wrote to Mum and Dad to get their agreement which obviously they gave as I was told if things were 'quiet' in London I would spend a short time at home before being transferred to Kettering in Northamptonshire where my new school was based.

I don't remember much about the interim, waiting to be transferred from the South to the Midlands, except I went through a spate of stealing, sweets mostly, although I wasn't above picking up a pencil or rubber in school and pretending it was mine. Sweets were on ration, a few ounces per person each week. Auntie Nellie bought our collective allowance on Saturdays and kept it in a tin on the larder shelf, to be given out fairly – but not very fairly, Pamie Glascock always got more – between us evacuees. Added to this a lady who lived in a big house some distance away saved her allowance and gave it to us. Every now and again I would be sent to collect it. Walking back carrying a sizable brown paper bag full of such 'goodies' was too much for me. While I would never have dreamt of stealing from the tin – I might have got caught, snitched on by one of the others, made to own up when some were found to be missing. But what was the harm in sampling a little of what was in that bag? A small bar of chocolate, a couple of pear drops, a sherbet dip. On one occasion I chose a gob-stopper, which lasted the whole of the long walk back and wasn't finished by the time I reached the house. To my disappointment the others were watching for me at the gate and I had to surreptitiously drop the remaining sliver of delicious taste in the hedge. After that I stuck to chocolate or dolly mixtures.

Going to Confession, as we were made to do every Saturday was difficult for me. Oh, that guilt again! I always tried to get Father Rae, much kinder and less judgmental than the other priest, whose name I forget. Even so, I seemed to spend more time on my knees saying my penance than the other kids. I always seemed to be the last one to leave the Church even though I was one of the first to arrive, to 'get it over with'. Most seemed to get away with one 'Our Father' and one 'Hail Mar' or three 'Hail Marys'. I often got a whole decade of the Rosary and once, when I admitted to rebellious thoughts and telling lies in my list of misdemeanours, the whole Rosary, all five decades of one of the Mysteries. I was told to dwell on the Five Sorrowful Mysteries where I would find, when comparing my lot with that of the Saviour, I had nothing to be rebellious about and was increasing His suffering by my selfishness. Guilt again – and more rebellious thoughts.

The transition from Dorset to Northamptonshire took place at the end of the Summer holidays. I recall being put on a train in the care of a guard, told to behave myself, look after my luggage (the same suitcase) and keep my gas-mask with me at all times. My father would meet me at Paddington. I worried all through the journey in case he wasn't there. What if there was an air-raid? What if they'd been bombed-out and were living in a refuge and didn't know I was coming? What if they were dead? As the train slowed on entering the great, grey, smelly London station I had pulled down the window and had my head sticking out – something I had been told, very emphatically, not to do. I had been given a graphic description of what had happened to a man who had stuck his head out at the wrong moment as a train entered a tunnel. My anxiety at the thought of my father not being there to meet me was obviously greater than the fear of losing my head in such a violent manner! Dad was there at the barrier.

The time spent in London with Mum, Dad and Pam before being sent off again is a bit of a blur. I remember the sounds, the drone of the planes, the rat-a-tat of the guns, the whistle of the bombs and the bangs and crashes as direct hits and gas explosions took place all around us. A couple of incidents stand out clearly, like when two little boys we knew were carried out of the wreckage. Terry and Johnny Cox, aged six and four. I thought they didn't look dead, only asleep, and half expected them to be out playing later in the day. Then there was the soldier returning on leave. He was walking along the street swinging his kit-bag, whistling. Coming to a patch of bombed-out buildings he suddenly stopped and looked bewildered. He continued walking, slowly and then stopped at a flight of steps, leading nowhere. He sat down on a lower step, placing his kit-bag carefully beside him. he was still there when I passed him again sometime later. I was told that he sat there, on the steps of his old house, for hours until someone led him away. His wife and children had been in the house when it had taken a direct hit.

I remember, too, my mother's 'premonitions'. For some reason – maybe because it was known she was part Gypsy – people took notice when Mum was troubled about something, even Dad, who was not by any means a fanciful man. Two occasions stand out. One was when Mum, for no apparent reason, told me to go and tell a neighbour she *must go to the shelter that night.* Lou and Don Cox (not related to little Terry and Johnny) had a horde of children, none of whom were evacuated. There were Coxes in every class in the school, plus a couple of older ones and a baby and toddler. They hardly ever went to a shelter, preferring to stay in their own cellar. I conveyed the message and the whole Cox family, with the exception of Patsy and Theresa, the two eldest congregated in the street shelter at the end of our road along with those of us who couldn't face the walk to the Tube. These shelters had very little space and most of the night was spent sitting on hard benches. They were more for sheltering from shrapnel and falling debris than for protection from bombs. During the night the baby was fretful and Lou sent Don back home to get some more gripe water. Don returned minutes later, shocked and dazed. Their home, together with half the street, was rubble. A similar thing happened when Mum suddenly decided we were to move. We were living in two rooms in the top floor of a house in Raddington Road, just off Portobello Road. Mum found a place to let in Hewer Street, an improvement on where we were because it had running water and its own toilet. Mum insisted we move there and then, using an old pram to convey our few possessions. Once there Pamie was crying for an old rag doll Dad had won for her at the Fair. I was sent back for it. The house, No 5, was gone, along with Mrs Hower, the landlady, and her son Johnny. Chance? Coincidence? I don't know. Hearsay? Definitely not. I was there.

Mum and Dad were always in poor health, Mum, frail from a tiny premature baby and Dad from frequent bouts of tuberculosis which sometimes took him away to a sanatorium. Real poverty and unemployment with no Welfare State were everyday matters. I remember Dad getting washed and shaved in the morning 'to look decent' and telling us he was going to 'watch the traffic lights change colour'. For a long time I thought that was a job. What he actually was doing was queuing at the Labour Exchange along with other unemployed men in the hope of a day's work sweeping the streets or bagging coal and coke to load on the coalman's carts, pulled by the large dray horses, who delivered most of the goods in those days. He came home whistling when he'd been working with the horses – happy for that little link with the countryside where he felt he belonged but where there was no work of any kind for someone in such poor health.

Mum, with Pam and I, would go to the Relief Office to get a slip of paper which entitled us to free food from the grocer, butcher etc. Long ago but not so far away.

We didn't know much about Mum's background. Granddad Goody didn't talk about his first wife, Mum's mother. Mum was nine years old when her mother died along with hew newly-born child, Teresa, leaving Mum to care for several little ones until Granddad married again and she was sent into service. There were tales of her mother coming from a family of Gypsies, but whether from the encampment at Pottery Lane Fields or the one at East London near where Mum was born, we never knew. It was said she brought skills with her: like the ones she used to save Mum who was a premature baby weighing only a couple of pounds and given up for dead. Her mother was said to have wrapped her in cotton wool, put her inside an earthenware jug placed among crumpled newspapers on the kitchen table and fed her hourly with milk in a fountain-pen dropper. Mum's diminutive size and frail health seemed to confirm the premature birth. Few premature babies survived in the early 1900's. So if Mum was troubled or gave a warning we, and neighbours we were friendly with, listened. I'm sure there must have been times when her 'premonitions' came to nothing. But her superstitions were often self-fulfilling. One of her superstitions came true over and over again.

Dor, uncross those knives. There'll be a row.

Of course there won't – don't be so superstitious.

I tell you – there'll be a row.

That's rubbish. You're being ridiculous.

Don't talk to your mother like that!

But Dad, she can't possibly believe …

What do you know about anything?

That's not fair, George. She's a clever girl, our Doreen. She knows a lot, from all those books she read.

Book-learning! Where did that every get you? Schools should teach them something practical, something that will help her get a decent job.

Then I wouldn't go to school.

You have to, it's the Law.

Well I don't care.

Don't answer back.

On and on. Of course there was a row.

Once again I was put on a train, this time with a newer, larger suitcase, care of the Guard and a bigger girl, Audrey somebody, who was also travelling to my new school. Mum saw me off this time. She talked a lot to this older girl, making her promise to look after me, as if I was a little one. I resented that and couldn't wait for the whistle to blow and the train to get going. Of course once it did I wanted her back to say goodbye properly – or, better still, to take me home again. The journey to Kettering passed in a mixture of misery and silent rebellion. Mum, Dad and my sister and Lou Cox's family were all still alive and well in London. Why not me? I tried not to think of Terry and Johnny. Or the soldier.

The Midland town of Kettering I remember in patches. Different billets, with people who complained I was too quiet, remote, well-behaved but unresponsive. One placing I recall clearly. I had been placed with a Mr and Mrs Tansy. He was a policeman of sorts – a Special Constable, I think. One day a tramp came to the back door and Mrs Tansy invited him in and gave him tea and cake. She told me I should stay and talk to him while he rested, she had things to do. As he cupped his hands around his mug of tea he started to tell me about how he had served in the trenches in the last way. 'Just a boy, I was,' he said. He was shaking as he talked, splodging tea down his front and I thought perhaps he would manage better if he took off his gloves. I was thinking how kind Mrs Tansy was when Mr Tansy came home accompanied by two other policemen, who immediately arrested the old man and dragged him off, not even letting him finish his tea. I couldn't see what he had done wrong. Apparently begging and being 'of no fixed abode' was crime enough. I thought they were terrible people and became even more distant, resulting in yet another move.

Around this time I spent quite a bit of time in hospital, not because I was ill but because there was nowhere else to put me and the Children's Homes were full. Towards the end of my evacuation I did spend one short period in one of these homes and hated it.

Hospital was fine though. I was happy there and wished I could stay. So much so that when I had a bit of stomach pain I pretended it was worse than it was – a girl at school had recently had appendicitis and had spent three weeks in hospital. I thought I would do the same – I must have been very convincing because it worked. I was rushed in and operated on. 'Ouch!' I hadn't wanted pain like that! The old adage 'beware of what you wish for' came home to roost. I learned my lesson. I have never faked anything since.

After that I had genuine causes for stays in hospital, with problems with walking, and accidents. One accident is still strange to look back upon as I have no memory of the actual happening whatsoever, only afterwards. There were two of us billeted with an elderly lady, a Mrs Blissett. I was about eleven, the other girl, also a Doreen, about seven or eight. Mrs Blessett had gone upstairs for a lie-down, with instructions to me to 'look after the younger one and to be sure to keep the fire in.' The open fire had been left banked-up, with the poker stuck in it to help it 'pull'. After a while the flames started to lick up the chimney. The end of the poker could be seen glowing red-hot. I left the Ludo game I had been playing, somewhat reluctantly, with Doreen, and knelt on the hearth to put more coal on the now lively fire. The poker must have shifted as I knelt down, probably the hook catching on the edge of my skirt. I knew nothing of this, felt nothing, until I became aware of the other girl screaming. I wondered what was the matter and tried to stand up. Only then did I realise that I had knelt on the poker. I do not remember experiencing any pain but passed out. The pain came in in full force when I regained consciousness in hospital. That was quite a long stay, several weeks, I think, as the burn 'through to the bone' took a long time to heal, leaving a deep, wide scar, faded now but still evident. I never had a visit, nor even a message, from Mrs Blissett, or Doreen. I never saw them again. Of course, on my discharge from hospital there was yet another 'home' to get used to.

For a while I was in Mansfield Orthopaedic Hospital, Northampton, undergoing foot surgery. I had always had trouble with my feet and back, conditions which had been put down to rickets. I had exercises for the slight curvature of the spine but it had been decided that surgery might correct the serious flat feet problem. One of the teachers from my school, Miss Russell who taught Latin, came to see me fairly regularly. We talked, of all things, about ballet, as she was a great ballet fan. She bought me a book of ballet, a big, yellow hard-back, with photos of the great dancers, which I treasured for years. She brightened up the day when she came and I remember her with affection. The interim times, with callipers and crutches, did nothing to improve my chances of being accepted into people's homes as a desirable evacuee. This led to the Children's Home episode as a lady complained my callipers tore her sheets. This may have been so but we were in the era of 'make do and mend', her sheets, as most people's, were already multi-patched and turned outside-edge to middle. I didn't see why I should be blamed and I expect I showed my resentment. She also stole my rolled gold cross and chain Mum and Dad had bought me. At first I believed her when she said I must have lost it, until I saw her daughter wearing it. She said her daughter had like it so much she had bought her one just like it. I was glad to go.

Mostly my memories of this time are patchy. Various billets, temporary stop-overs, occasional days-out to Wicksteed Park for a treat with people I didn't know, the highlight of which was a ride down the water-shute. I wondered why I couldn't stay with kindly people like these. I spent a lot of time 'in my head' day-dreaming, making up stories to myself, sometimes writing them down. I liked to be by myself, and would walk to Weekly Woods, and wander over the iron-ore quarry, imagining past-and-future-scenarios. I climbed trees and sat for hours in a lower branch, just thinking. On one occasion I must have dozed and fell out into the pool below. I had to walk back soggy and muddy to a 'good telling off'. I think, perhaps, I wasn't an easy child!

There was a lot of talk about the war ending soon, of returning to blitzed and battered London – and to our families.

After the War

Of course there were some who had no family to go back to. And some who had families who didn't want them back. And some who didn't want to go back. In the weeks leading up to that journey 'home' I remember trying to piece together what I would be going back to. My memory of 'before' at that time was sketchy – I can recall that pre-war era much better now. I had pictures in my head of playing in the street: tying skipping-rope to the arms of the lamppost and swinging round it, hop-scotch, whip-and-top, marbles, trying to win a 'kingy', jumping on the back of the rag-and-bone man's horse-drawn cart to get a ride, with passers-by, usually other kids not quite as brave, calling out 'Look behind, Mister!' and running like hell whenever he stopped, always looking after little Pam, not letting her do some of the things I liked doing in case she got hurt and I would get into trouble. Mum used to go to work very early in the mornings, to scrub the corridor floors of Du Cane Road hospital. In the times when Dad wasn't at home because he was in the Sanatorium with tuberculosis I was in charge of getting myself and Pam up and off to school. Sometimes Mum was back by the time we came home, sometimes not, so I let us in with the key on a string behind the letter box. Weekends, if Dad was home, saw both of us sitting on the steps of the Eagle pub on a weekend night, hoping for a bag of crisps with a blue packet of salt, while Mum and Dad had a Guinness.

I knew it could not be like that now. To start with I was older, almost fourteen, and none of these things, if they still existed, would be open to me. Mum and Dad and my sister were still there, but, if not exactly strangers, not really familiar either. Dad went to work now, a proper job with a decorator's firm, and Mum, and Pam, now eleven, were mates rather than mother and daughter. They did each other's hair, went to the pictures together, liked the same films and film stars. They didn't read, except for the 'News of the World' on a Sunday and thought I was either destined to be clever (in the light of the Grammar School Scholarship) or not right in the head because I did. I read anything and everything, from textbooks and library books, Persian poetry (in translation), Don Quixote, crime and romance, to Enid Blyton, Radio Fun and the Beano. I loved Hiawatha and read it so much I almost knew it by heart, and remember much of it still. 'Dor's no company', my mother would complain, 'always got her head in a book.' When I hadn't got my head in a book I could be found down the road at the Co-op dairy. They stabled the horses there. Large dray horses that pulled the milk carts. About 5a.m. each morning we would hear them clip-clopping past as they set off to deliver the milk. I loved those horses and after school I would go down to the stables to help groom them. One, a big strawberry roan, called Strawberry, was my favourite. She was very affectionate and would nuzzle me and stamp her foot when I had to leave. Other times would find me along with the other local kids poking around in the rubble all around us looking for shrapnel and bits of bombs. Most of us had quite a collection which, as we were still on rations, would often be traded for sweet coupons or clothing coupons which could then be traded for other scarce necessities. Not everyone could afford to buy all the goods for which they had the requisite number of coupons, so there was quite a brisk use of coupons as currency.

My parents were a bit puzzled about the Scholarship and I think not sure how to deal with it. In their world children left school at fourteen, after picking up the essentials of reading, writing and arithmetic which they agreed were essential, to go to work. You earned your crust. We understood that if you didn't work in some way, you didn't eat. Even as little ones, before the war, we had earned: cleaning doorsteps with scrubbing brush and hearthstone, running errands, taking messages and taking the pennies home to Mum. When Dad came home from the Sanatorium and he had casual work, sometimes for a day, sometimes longer, things were better and we occasionally could buy a treat with our contribution: a bag of broken biscuits, some black-jacks – or jelly and custard for tea. But here was I, going on fourteen, being kitted out with uniform and books to continue to attend school in September, and expected to remain there until I would go to University at eighteen. Although I got a Grant to cover my school fees, and a separate one for uniform, books and travelling – the school was some distance away, necessitating a twice-daily trip on the Underground – it was going to be difficult for them. But for that first year back from evacuation there was no choice as, just the previous year, a Government Act had raised the school leaving age to fifteen.

I was disappointed. I would have liked to go to work. Although I liked most of the lessons (except Maths) and enjoyed learning, I disliked school. I always had from the beginning. Before the war I would frequently dawdle on the way, making Pam and I late. There was a lady at the corner of our street who had a large number of cats and I would stop until I had stroked as many as possible. It could take a long time on a wet, drizzly day when the cats didn't want to be enticed from the shelter of the doorway to the railings. I didn't dare go behind the gate as rumour had it that she was a witch.

But I couldn't get away with such procrastinations now. I had trains to catch. There were consequences to face for lateness: extra time to put in, cancelled lunch-breaks, detentions – even on Saturday mornings. And there was the dreaded daily Assembly during which any deserved accolades were given and all shaming done before the whole school. Each morning before the start of lessons three hundred and sixty or so girls would line up, six Form-lines, facing the stage on which sat the teachers, most of them nuns. In the centre in front of the row of chairs stood the formidable figure of Mother Catherine, the Head. The teachers sat throughout unless one of them was called upon to give comment. We pupils stood. Occasionally, usually if the proceedings had been somewhat lengthy, someone fainted and was quietly assisted to the chairs at the side of the Hall. Mother Catherine was the ultimate deterrent to bad behaviour of any kind. The slightest misdemeanour, even a look which could be interpreted as 'insolent', was treated with as much severity as serious deliberate infringement. We were all 'above the Age of Reason' (seven) and therefore culpable. We were all making *choices* and we had to be sure that those we made were *approved* choices or we would be in big trouble!

We had a system of Plus Marks and Fault Marks given for everything from excellent or bad work, attitude (good or bad), running in the corridors and, of course, lateness for school (never mind delays on the Tube and buses and the weather), lessons, Chapel and detention. Once a week, on Friday mornings, there would be a summary, Form by Form, of the girl with the most Plus Marks and the girl with the most Fault marks, who as her name was called would go to the platform and stand beside Mother Catherine, Plus Marks on her right, Fault Marks on her left. It happened on one occasion the same girl qualified for both. Me. Perhaps it happened on other occasions, it must have, but I only remember the one.

Plus Marks first. 'Lower Fourth – Doreen Frost. Well done, child. Keep it up.'

'Thank-you Mother.' I took my place beside the top-of-the-class girl in pig-tails from the Upper Third Form. The rest of the Forms followed. Then to the Fault Marks. Two Third Forms, with naughty little Patsy Laslett from the Upper Third there again, trying not to giggle and earn herself yet another black mark. I remember a queasy feeling in my stomach, a sense of foreboding for I knew I had been in trouble quite a bit with various teachers during the previous week. The moment came. That moment when you *know* all the stars are going to fall from the sky. The moment when the floor will cave in and you will disappear forever. The moment when Mother Catherine's voice boomed out 'Lower Fourth – Doreen Frost,' and I had to walk the long death-walk around the back of our mammoth Mother Superior to emerge, as from the dark side of the moon, on her left side. There was a titter, then open laughter allowed to run its course unchecked, at the end of which she reached out behind Patsy and grabbed my arm, pulling me beside her.

'The place of honour, I think! Wait outside my Office after Assembly. We need to have a little talk.' More tittering, cut off this time by an imperious lift of the hand, everyone glad it was me and not them. As I would have been, if only.

Schooldays, as I have said, were not the Happiest Days of my Life. Some years later, in the 1950's, when the film 'The Happiest Days of Your Life' came out I thought John Dighton, the playwright had got it all wrong. Had he never been to school?

Yes, much of it was interesting and occasionally some of it was fun but from the first day the feeling of being in some alien element persisted. I never felt I belonged there. But I wanted to learn so I began to ask questions – frequently it seemed, the wrong questions. Religion was the worst danger zone. 'If being a Catholic was the only way to get into Heaven why were so many people born in areas that had never heard of Christianity? And why were so many Christians Protestants? What about all the people who had never been, nor could ever be reached by the bearers of the life-saving message – were they all doomed to eternal damnation? And how fair was that, from a supposedly loving God? If Adam and Eve were the first people had they had two sons, Cain and Able, where did the rest of the human race come from? Did God approve incest?' We had no sex education but we knew from the Church's rule forbidding cousins to marry, that in-breeding was unhealthy and unlawful. 'Be quiet, child, and get on with your work. Get yourself to Confession – may God forgive you for having such thoughts in your head.' More Fault Marks and once a suspension. 'Get yourself home, girl, and think of the sinful path you are on. Come back after you've made a good Confession.' I went back because I had to, but unrepentant. The threat of eternal hellfire was forever being held over us as just punishment for 'wicked thoughts'. Chastity was a word we Convent girls heard often.

'Chastity, the Virtue of Virtues. Pictures of St. Agnes, as pure as the lamb she carried in her arms, popped up everywhere:

hung on the wall in the corridor, in the doorway of the school Chapel, given as Holy Pictures for our prayer books.

'Be careful, girls. There is temptation around every corner, even tucked up in your beds at night. Always sleep with your arms by your sides. Never let your *hands* or your *thoughts* wander. Keep *pure* girls. *C.H.A.S.T.E.* girls. Be *chaste* as our Blessed Mother Mary and holy St. Agnes were chaste. Some, never strong on spelling, misread this *CHASED*.

Enlightened by the whispered details of their adventures with boys, our thinking underwent a Road to Damascus experience. Chastity no longer lived amongst us. I suspect I'm still booked in for an eternity of Hell-fire for that one!

English was another difficult area. I've always loved the written word and enjoyed writing essays and compositions but sadly in my first year at such a prestigious school I had a teacher who did not appreciate my efforts. Given a title, 'Pictures in the fire' I was delighted, thinking I could really go to town on that. I worked hard on it, checking all grammar, punctuation and syntax and felt it was well-written. I usually got A or A- for my work, but this time it was returned with 'see me' scrawled on it in red ink. I was told I must learn to *curb my imagination*! The same comment, also written in red, was put on my school report. I was, in today's parlance, gobsmacked!

As I have said, I couldn't wait to leave school. Academically I was doing well enough and was told I was heading for Oxford (our school's Mecca) but I did not want to go to University. I wanted to go to work, to leave home, and to continue my education at evening classes and from reading, reading, reading. Home was becoming an increasingly difficult place to be. I did not understand the world Mum, Dad and Pam lived in – but I expected them to understand, or at least accept, mine. Going to the pictures once or twice a week, whatever was showing; hanging round the pub on a Friday night while Dad had his pint and Mum her Guinness, always smoking, reading the 'News of the World' somehow held no attraction for me. I wanted something else, but I didn't know what. I loved them dearly, felt very protective of them, and knew they loved me, but again, was aware of that feeling of not quite belonging.

Sometimes we visited within the family. Mum had a sister, my Auntie Rose, and we would visit her and my Uncle Charlie, who kept pigeons in a shed in his backyard. I liked Uncle Charlie and on these occasions I would spend most of my time with him and the pigeons. Uncle Charlie would tell wonderful tales of how clever pigeons are, how they carried messages through the Great War, how loving they were to their partners and young. I thought they were beautiful and loved the way they would sit on my hand, cock their heads to one side and appear to talk to me. Pam played with our cousin Lionel, who she adored and followed everywhere while Mum and Auntie Rose chatted through endless pots of tea, sharing their views on life through a haze of Woodbine smoke. Mum also had half-brothers and their families nearby, especially Uncle Charlie, her favourite, (Charlie Grey, not Charlie Rowntree, Aunt Rose's husband) and his wife Peggy. Dropping in at their basement flat in Elgin Crescent there was always a welcome and a cup of tea. Mum's father, Albert Goody, with his second wife, Leiley, and their daughter Eileen, still lived in Clarendon Road, where Pam and I had been born. Eileen was only marginally older than me but, apart from lending me her First Communion dress when I was seven, I remember very little about her. We all, irreverently but affectionately, knew Granddad Goody as 'Billy-born-drunk'. Not that we ever saw him drunk. We children usually saw him in his shoe-repair shop where we would stand and watch him cutting and shaping leather, fitting shoes on to different sized lasts, hammering nails in, one at a time, from a collection lined up between his lips. We waited nervous and excited, for him to swallow one, but he never did. At home on a Sunday he would be sitting in his arm-chair reading 'The News of the World', a large glass of Guinness within reach and an unopened bottle on the floor beside him. In later years when they had a television he was heard to say that when he died he wanted to go watching the football while having a Guinness. And so he did, one Saturday afternoon, the almost-empty glass placed carefully on the floor beside him, still touched by his out-stretched hand.

Dad's family mostly lived in Essex, around the Tilbury area, so we didn't see much of them. Granddad Frost was a stern old man. I didn't like him much but I was fond of Grandma, who was an invalid after she had a stroke and spent her days on the sofa in the tiny cottage's living room. Granddad had a garden in which he grew vegetables and salads – he thought it was a waste of good ground to grow anything you couldn't eat. He sold his produce to family and passers-by, charging family slightly more because, he said, as they picked their own they would select the best! He was probably right, but it didn't do much to endear him to us. There were lots of aunts and cousins around. The ones I like most were my father's brother, Uncle Denis, Auntie Myrtle and their daughter Mary. Mary and I remained friends right into adulthood, until she died recently in her late seventies.

Two of Dad's sisters, Babs and Dora, lived in London. We visited them occasionally. Babs was a gentle, kindly woman married to an artist called Percy Laurante who had a studio shop in Westbourne Grove, where he painted local scenes from sketches, St Stephen's Church, the canal, and did lacquer work on items of furniture. Uncle Percy was colourful, flamboyant and fun. Children liked him and he liked them. The shop was always full of local children watching him work. I loved going over there but Mum and Dad didn't like them much, calling Percy 'the Great I Am' and they fell out with them over their son Ronnie stealing our ration books. The falling out was hardly surprising as Mum took him to court and he was found guilty. I felt that it wasn't their fault that their son had committed the unforgivable sin – robbing his own – so continued to visit them and they always made me welcome but Mum and Dad broke off all contact until some years later Ronnie, with his wife Sadie, came to say how sorry he was. No longer the wild, wayward, 'delinquent' lad, Ronnie had turned into quite a nice young man and was forgiven. Mum always said that her taking him to court had steadied him and maybe it had. But I don't remember Mum and Dad ever visiting Babs and Percy again.

Auntie Dora lived in Finsbury Park and invited us over from time to time. She was known to be fairly well-off, owning property, a car and taking several holidays a year to places like Switzerland and Jersey. I remember one year, just after the War, we were all thrilled when we were invited for Christmas. At that time we had never had a proper Christmas Dinner, a rabbit stew was the height our celebrations had ever reached. Dad was still unemployed and there was still strict rationing. That dinner at Auntie Dora's and Uncle Cyril's house was memorable, not least because as we were thanking them profusely for their kindness, Dora presented Dad with a bill for his share of the meal! As we were four and they were two she wanted Dad to pay the lion's share! I like her even less than I like Granddad Frost! Uncle Cyril, who was a gentle, kindly man, tried to argue with her, but he was no match for his domineering self-serving wife. We still visited them from time to time, Dad paying, bit by bit, what he 'owed' but I never went willingly, making every excuse I could think up and stopped altogether as soon as I could get away with it.

Sunday mornings were the best time for me. If the weather was fine Dad and I would walk up to 'The Plough' on the corner of Ladbroke Grove and Harrow Road, where there was always a cockle and whelk stall outside and, along the side, a man sold plants. Like most of the back-to-back tenements we had a bit of a backyard but Dad and I had turned it into a garden. Dad had made spaces in the concrete so we had a small lilac tree, an apple tree and along one side we had runner beans climbing up the wall with a few flowers between. I loved those times, talking plants with the man, having a plate of cockles then coming home and grubbing around with Dad in the little planting space we had, talking about all we could do if we had a real garden. Dad's heart was always in the country. Another thing we shared, which remains a life-long passion, is a love of opera. When I was very young, around three or four, Dad had some casual work in a wine cellar with some Italians and came home singing their songs. Because he was very dark he identified with them and fancied he had Mediterranean blood in his background. Whether he had or not we never discovered, but that did not deter him from using his very pleasant voice to bring their music home with him. I loved these Neapolitan songs and operatic arias and as I grew older would fiddle around, much to my Mother's annoyance, trying to find them on the radio. That way, tracking the foreign wave-bands, I discovered opera and longed to have a gramophone so I could play the records without having to listen through all that static. Later, with Caruso and Gigli, Richard Tauber and

Joseph Locke, it became more popular here and we had it on the ordinary radio so reception was better.

Dad and I also liked going to the pictures together. Sometimes we went as a fmily, walking together along Ladbroke Grove to the other side of Harrow Road, seeing whatever was on at the two cinemas there, getting a bag of chips at the Fish and Chip shop as we passed on the way home. Other times Dad and I would go further afield, taking the bus up to Notting Hill Gate to see, perhaps a foreign film or something with a serious theme that did not appeal to Mum or Pam. They liked lots of Hollywood glamour, romance and known stars, which we also enjoyed but we liked stories which touched on the dark side too. One film Dad and I saw together, The African Queen, was a combination of the two; two great but certainly not glamorous stars, Humphrey Bogart and Kathryn Hepburn, love, romance but with dark undertones of war. We said we would love to see it again and regretted not going to the earlier showing. In those days the cinemas started showing around mid-day and went on continuously until ten-thirty or so at night. Once inside you could stay as long as you liked so it didn't matter if you arrived in the middle of a feature, you could stay until you came to where you came in. And if you wished you could see the whole programme round again, staying until the National Anthem, when everybody stood at respectful attention before the mad scramble for the exit doors. That all stopped, including the standing for 'The King' or, later, 'The Queen', when they introduced an interval between showings with different start times. On the way home we said we would see if it was showing somewhere nearby – perhaps in Paddington or South Kensington – the following week. We would go again, even though it would cost more to go to a 'posh' cinema. The African Queen was the last film

Dad and I saw together. He died, after a long bout of illness and incapacity, in 1954 aged only forty-eight. I still feel the pang of loss when that old film pops up, as it does from time to time, as a glorious 'oldie' on television.

Mum didn't understand my love of books and music. But she, too, loved to sing – but not along with Dad. She knew all the old Music Hall songs as well as all the current favourites on the radio. And she could play the piano after a fashion, to accompany herself, 'vamping' she called it. She had never had a lesson, but probably picked it up as a child – every home with the space had a piano – or while in service. She had never been to a play or a concert but had memories of a pantomime, which had left her with dreams of 'going on the stage'. Maybe if permanent ill-health and desperate poverty had not barred her way she may have done so.

I enjoyed shopping so Mum and I would go 'down the Lane' (Portobello Market) together, she carrying an old oil-cloth shopping-bag in one hand and her handbag in the other. I had an eye for a bargain and enjoyed getting more for our money that we had expected. I knew many of the stall-holders, most of whom were pleasant and cheery and would often throw in a little bit extra: an apple, a couple of onions, a bit of boiled beetroot. In those days it was quite customary to see a big steaming pot on the side of a vegetable stall cooking fresh beetroots.

Shopping had not always been such an enjoyable experience. I have memories of a couple of scary experiences before the war. I would wander through the market hoping to pick up any stray items: an apple, a potato, discarded cabbage or cauliflower leaves, anything to 'add to the pot'. When Mum was with me she would pretend not to notice. On one occasion I was on my own and dawdled beside a fruit and vegetable stall. The produce was piled high in beautiful, colourful pyramids. Nearest me a mountain of large, shiny apples. The thought of a luscious, juicy unblemished and unbruised apple was too much for me. I reached out and surreptitiously took hold of one. In an instant, it seemed, the whole known world did a somersault. A cascade poured off the barrow and went racing down the road which sloped towards the lower end of the Market. King Edward potatoes with the pink blush on them, carrots, swedes, turnips, parsnips, onions, tomatoes and little shallots all rolled and bounced away from the irate, screaming, dancing stall-holder. I ran, still clutching the apple, along the road and around the corner, reaching the safety of home without being grabbed by a passer-by or feeling the hand of a policeman on my shoulder. Looking at my stolen fruit I found I couldn't eat it. I gave it to Pam, telling Mum a lady had given it to me, thus receiving unearned praise for being generous and kind! Oh dear. That guilt again! For a long time after, I was afraid to pass that stall in case anyone recognised me. I would cross over the road to pat a dog or look in a shop window.

I especially liked the bookstalls. One, right at the top, Notting Hill end of the Market, was run by a really nice man called John. John had been crippled by polio which had distorted his spine and he walked with great difficulty, a lurching, twisted walk, using two sticks. But he was cheerful, saying wasn't he lucky he didn't have to go to work but could spend his time with his beloved books. I made great discoveries there, dipping into his second-hand books. He never minded me standing there for ages reading books I could not, at that time, hope to buy. I would go back again and again to finish something, or read another poem, hoping the book had not been sold in the meantime. I did not know about libraries. I discovered these wonderful bolt holes later, when looking for a refuge from street gangs on my way home from school. Standing out in my posh uniform I was like a flame to belligerent moths. So after school I would deliberately miss trains at Euston Square station so as to arrive at Ladbroke Grove at different times then scuttle quickly across the road to the Library to while away sufficient time for the easily-bored youths to move on to look for another victim. I don't think I was ever afraid of coming to any serious physical harm, they saved the cutting and disfiguring for ex-girl-friends who had betrayed them, but general harassment, verbal abuse, the wrecking of uniform – especially the hat and tie – destruction of books and homework were causes for great hilarity. The Library became my refuge from such torments. I still continued to go to John's stall in the Portobello long after I discovered the riches on the Library shelves. It was there, among John's books, that I discovered Kahlil Gibran, the Lebanese poet, whose thinking had a great influence on me, and Don Quixote at age fifteen, with whom I fell in love. I remember saying, when asked, that if I ever fell in love it would be with an idealist, a man with a head full of dreams and an unlined pocket. And so it was – and is.

Occasionally when shopping we would stop off at the 'pie and mash' shop. In my mind's eye I can still see it; a long shop with a serving counter along one side, behind which stood large cooking vats full of the green, steaming liquor in which the eels were cooked, containers of stewed eels, mashed potato and racks of meat pies. Along the opposite wall's length the tile-topped tables for four with benches along each side, each table topped with the obligatory salt, pepper and vinegar. Like fish-and-chip shops it had its own particular smell, taunting and tantalizing if you had to walk by without going on. On the rare days when Mum hesitated at the shop door Pam and I were in there like a shot, scrambling for a place to sit, keeping a place for Mum as she checked her purse before going to the counter. Pam and I would have a meat pie of indeterminate identity with mash and parsley sauce eel-liquor, if we could afford it, or just the mash and liquor if not. Mum invariably would have stewed eels with hers instead of the pie. Her idea of Heaven, I think, was a Guinness and a pot of jellied eels followed by a nice strong cup of tea and cigarette. It didn't take much to make her happy. Her husband, her two girls, and those little treats were all she asked for. Later, when I was nursing, after Dad had died of heart failure at forty-eight, I took Mum for several holidays. We booked a caravan at West Wittering in Sussex, then, a year or so later, on the Isle of Wight. Mum loved it – she had her Guinness, cigarettes and plenty of pots of tea but still the first thing she did on our return home was to pop off down Portobello for a plate of eels and mash! I could see why Dad had never been able to return to live in the country! He had talked for a time of emigrating to New Zealand to do sheep-farming. There was a scheme that would transport people for £10 a head. He applied but was turned down on health grounds – the same reason that he was not called up during the War. I remember his disappointment and sense of worthlessness. But he knew Mum would never have gone, and Dad, although he was capable of being unfaithful and frequently was, would never have left her.

The only bit of 'country' Mum appreciated was bird-life, especially sparrows. She said they were 'proper London birds' and identified with them, calling herself a 'cockney sparrer'. Born in Hoxton, within the sound of Bow Bells which authenticated the 'Cockney' identity she remained a genuine East-ender until her death, at fifty-three, in 1960. The emphysema which had plagued her all her short life caught up with her on Mothers' Day just a week before our first child, Jonathan, was born. How she fought to hang on to see that baby – convinced – hoping – it was a girl. My sister already had boys. Sadly Mum was never to be around to know our six lovely daughters who followed Jonathan. She and Dad have missed so much dying so young. I wish they could have lived into old age and experienced some of the modern benefits that I am fortunate to have now. I would have loved to have cared for them, watched Mum brushing the little girls' hairs, seen Dad at home in our lovely garden. I miss them still.

At fifteen I left school without sitting the School Certificate (equivalent to GCSEs now) or the more prestigious Matriculation Certificate, and went to work as I had wanted. My first job was in the local Day Nursery where I worked long, hard hours and learned a lot about very young children. Most evenings I would be at the theatre and weekends were spent doing voluntary work (mainly with the children) in the local school now being used as a refuge for war victims from the camps in Poland. Their stories still horrify me. In that era, immediately after the War, I met many survivors of that terrible time and have been greatly influenced by – awed by – their quiet courage and lack of bitterness as they faced once again the life they thought was finished. And the children, once settled in, with all they had seen and suffered, still smiled and laughed and played. I think I always had sympathy with people who had to struggle for their place in life. I hated anything I saw as injustice.

I had a few friends from school, but none very close, probably because we did not live near each other and rarely met outside the Convent's well-supervised confines where personal relationships were not encouraged. There was Pauline O'Rouke and her sister Sheila, whose father was killed on a London bus when its top was sliced off by a too-low bridge, Joanie Dineen who occasionally would meet me at the Serpentine for a paddle, (I was too scared of the water to attempt to swim. I was well into my fifties before I dared take my feet off the ground). I never knew where they lived and they never came to my house. Where are they now? I've no idea. We soon lost touch after I started work and they are now a shadowy memory, only barely visible because I am straining my eyes in their direction. Like so many others, not even ships that pass in the night, more like ships laid up in dry dock together for a short while, going nowhere.

We had friends across the road, Lou Crisp who was a good friends of Mum's, and her two daughters, Beatie and Violet, who lived nearby. Beatie and Violet were both married, Beatie with two small children, Robin and Lydia, and Violet with five. I saw Robin and Lydia often, visiting at least once most weeks, sometimes staying the night to give Beatie and her husband Don a break. Violet and her Italian husband never seemed to need a baby-sitter but I spent a lot of time sitting with the kids on the stone steps leading up to their front door telling them stories, inventing new games. Sometimes, if I was going anywhere special, like Oxford Street or Kensington High Street, I would take Vera, who was my favourite, with me. She loved those outings. I remember once giving a Christmas party for them in our basement flat. I decorated it, made lots of jellies and little cakes and sandwiches in the shape of animals and made 'lucky bags' containing a little gift and a few sweets, before, I think 'lucky bags' had been invented. The children were delighted – excepted for Robin, aged three, who was obviously unimpressed. He surveyed the scene critically, looked inside a sandwich to check the filling, and said firmly 'I don't want any. Have you got any giblet soup?'

I loved the children and thought how lucky old Mrs Crisp was to have such lovely grandchildren. And I liked Beatie and Vi. Although they were older than me we remained good friends over many years until their death and I am still in touch with the 'children', grandparents themselves now, to this day.

My closest friend at this time was Margaret Rose White, named after the princess, who was good at French and later married a Frenchman. Margaret lived across the road and went to a different school, Burlington High. We were the only two in our area to go to Grammar school so we suffered the same trials from street gangs – many of whom had been our friends on the street in earlier childhood. Margaret did not have to travel to school so was spared having to 'run the gauntlet' at the Tube station but she had her patches of torment on the way home just the same. Our school uniforms with the emblazoned blazer and panama hats, mine brown and gold, her navy and red, highlighted our suitability as victims. In the school holidays Margaret and I would go to Kensington High Street window-shopping together, enjoying the smart shops and window displays. Apart from the occasional tiny item, a scarf, a notebook, any real buying was done on the way back down the Portobello Road. As soon as I left school I moved away from home to take various living-in jobs as Mother's Help and Nursery Nurse. I went home every week on my day off, taking some of the money I'd earned to help Mum and usually met up with Margaret who had stayed on at school, becoming Head Girl and getting her Matriculation Certificate with distinction. She then went to France and met a man she was soon to marry. Margaret's Mum, Rose and my Mum were close friends and spent a lot of time together drinking endless pots of tea, sharing a Guinness and virtually chain-smoking. Their talk consisted mainly of 'pulling the feathers out' of their husbands, other people's husbands and men folk in general. They were not enamoured of the male sex and it appeared would cheerfully do without them. Until Rose lost her husband and Mum lost Dad. It all changed then, as did Rose and Mum. The eulogies were heartfelt but unheard by the focus of their tributes, the tears genuine and their grief more poignant because these things had not been said when it mattered. Poor Mum. Poor Rose. Margaret, apart from the Frenchman she had met, was not interested in boys but I had dates with various boyfriends whenever I had time. Usually we would go to the theatre, or a concert or the 'Proms' during the season, or to the New Lindsay Theatre Club where we would meet with other friends. And of course there was ballroom dancing. Everywhere had its weekend Dance. In days gone by we didn't go clubbing we went *dancing*. We learned the steps, quick-step, foxtrot, waltz, twist, rock-an'-roll practising to Victor Sylvester on the wireless. Then, on Saturday night, dressed up to the nines, off to the local Palais we went to sit pretending disinterest as the young men congregated at the far end of the hall near the band eyeing us up. Then the magic words 'May I have this dance?' Ah! The Dance was special then, anything could happen. It rarely did but there was always the possibility that just maybe … I liked dancing and I liked the idea of romance but always back off after one or two dates not wanting any closer involvement. I had made up my mind I did not want to marry. Pam was married, Mum and Dad had had a long marriage, none of them particularly happy with their state and Margaret, about to be married, seemed very middle-aged. That, I thought, was not for me.

Margaret and I still saw quite a lot of each other after the Slum Clearance drive moved us to an enormous flat in Powis Square, nearer to Notting Hill, but Mum and Rose, although only a few doors away from each other, never picked up on their old companionship again. Eventually Margaret moved to France and Rose moved away into a smaller place and we lost touch.

Mum missed Rose – and she missed Dad. She had a friend at the pub, a man called George Baker. He lived with his mother and had never been married. George was charming to Mum and gave her a lot of attention. Eventually he asked her to marry him and she agreed. Pam and I weren't sure how we felt about it. We didn't really like George Baker but we were sad to see Mum, in poor health, so alone and so reliant on us. I had been living at home looking after her for some time, going to and from the hospital at all hours for my shifts. I had applied to the W.H.O. for possible work in refugee camps as soon as I qualified and didn't see how I was going to be able to do that. Mum marrying would solve that for me. Pam, married, with a baby boy, Paul, couldn't be there all the time and could barely cope with Paul. So we each had our own selfish reasons for encouraging her to go ahead and try to fill that space that Dad had left. As it happened I was not to go to work with the refugees as I had planned because I met and fell in love with my future husband. Mum married George and I married and moved to Leicester to live with my husband's family.

Mum's marriage was a disaster. Very soon after George had moved in he started to show another side to his character. Mum was giving me reports of how he would always compare her unfavourably with his mother, how he would leave her alone for hours, preferring to go back to his mother's dingy basement flat, how he would spit in the food she put before him on the table and insult her. He pressured her to go and stay with her daughters and although fiery by nature she was too frail to put up much of a fight. So she came to us in Leicester. Having miscarried our first baby at nineteen weeks I was on complete bed rest with the second – from mid-August to late December 1959 – with the doctor calling every other day. We lived in the top two rooms of a house, with all facilities, including running water on the floor below. My husband, Pepe, worked at the shoe factory about a mile away and would run home in his lunch hour to see if we needed anything. Mum at least was on her feet, able to make tea and toast. I was unable to tackle the stairs so had to make do with a covered bucket in the bedroom. Pepe was wonderful, never complaining, and mainly through his care we managed to save this baby, our son Jonathan, who had been threatening to miscarry from the early days. It was to be five months before he was secure enough for me to be up and about. This was a difficult time for us so Mum decided she would go to Pam and Ronnie in Corby for a short visit before going home to sort out what she was going to do about George. He had made murmurings about moving his mother in to live in Mum's flat. Mum didn't want that to happen. As it turned out she didn't have to return to London. She went to Pam's in February, became ill with her usual bout of bronchitis and emphysema, went into kidney failure and died in Kettering Hospital on Mothers' Day in March. She would have been fifty-three in April. I managed to get to see her the week before she died. She was still more concerned with my health than her own. Drifting in and out of consciousness she was murmuring about the dangers of damp clothes and sitting in draughts. Several times when she was lucid she said she wasn't' going to make it. I was back being a daughter again. Not the little girl daughter, where Mummy could kiss everything better, make everything right again. The growing-up, know-it-all, Mum's got it wrong, daughter.

'I think your old Mum's cracking up, Dor,' she'd said. 'Of course you're not' I told her, more sharply than I intended. 'You'll be right as rain when the better weather comes. You always are.' The optimistic daughter, protecting herself from the reality of mortality. Mum wasn't old enough to 'crack up', I was married and our first child was due any day. Mum had always been ailing, why should this time be any different? Thinking of that time, the last time I saw her, I thought how horrible I must have seemed, how unsympathetic, how uncaring. But even when my head, the trained nurse in me, told me the truth, I still could not believe she was going to die. It has taken me many years to allow myself to give up feelings of guilt for thing I could not help: The War; me being sent away – and Mum dying without me realizing she was dying but was hanging on to see the baby. She so wanted it to be a girl. Her funeral took place a week before Jonathan was born. Pepe went by train in my place, as the baby, already three weeks late was imminent. I wanted to be there, to say 'goodbye' but having lost one, had to do as I was told and put the safety of the baby first. I know when I last saw her she was dying but somehow whenever I have walked down Portobello Road since I have still half-expected to see her toddling along, carrying her Liberty's oil-cloth shopping bag.

At her funeral George Baker was nowhere in evidence and we never heard from him or of him again.

One friend I did keep in touch with, through all the years and all the changes, was Margarita Marsh, know to us as Margery. Margery was the 'big girl' who had talked to me as

I sat on our steps before the war, the 'big sister' of the rather delicate little boy, David, who I was asked to keep an eye on in school when we both started at St. Charles' together. On my return from evacuation David and I met up again and became close, supporting each other through teenage traumas. I learned later that everyone, including his mother and sister, expected us to marry. The only people who didn't think of it and accept it as a forgone conclusion were David and I! I thought of him more as the brother I didn't have and he poured his heart out to me over various girls and his dream of playing cricket. Our relationship never came into it. I started to visit Margery, married and expecting her first baby. We became firm friends. I knitted her first layette of baby clothes, baby-sat for her when the children, Philip and Martin, were small, played with them, took them out, told them stories. Her husband, Ted, a London taxi-driver, was seldom there. Margery's house in Golborne Road became my second home. Even after I had left home, all through the changes the following years brought, nursing, marriage, children, we maintained that friendship and she became a very important person in my children's lives. She remembered birthdays, Christmas and was always interested in their achievements, always made us welcome, as did the boys as they grew up. Margery is gone now, leaving us with a sense of loss no-one could ever fill. But we still think of the boys, now middle-aged men, as family. It was largely due to Margery that years later we became house owners. We had moved from Wales where Pepe had been at college and were living in a council house in Grays in Essex with our seven young children. Pepe had his first teaching job at Torells, a local Secondary School, soon to become a greatly enlarged Comprehensive. Margery and Ted, on selling their house in London (for what seemed to us, and them, a vast sum) to make their longed-for move to the country, gave us a gift of £500.

An enormous sum to us. £90 went on much needed home improvement – three separate little beds for the eldest children – leaving £410 untouched. What to do with such a bonanza!? House buying, with 10% deposit and interest at 14% was out of the question. Or was it? I visited the Council and persuaded them that it would be in their interest to give us a 100% mortgage, so releasing a large council house and them from their obligation to continue to house our large family. The money we had would pay the solicitors and other expenses. We got our mortgage and bought a house in Highview Avenue. We were on the housing ladder, feeling that our greatly appreciated gift from our dearly-loved friend was well-spent.

After my return from evacuation I became very interested in the Theatre and joined an amateur group based at the 'Twentieth Century' Theatre, in Westbourne Grove. I didn't really want to act so much as write and direct, but I had to do whatever was needed which was mainly being a general dogsbody and filling in small parts that nobody else wanted. I also gathered together a small group, wrote little plays and we performed them in the park and at the Community Centre. Later, when I was writing and producing my own plays for my Children's Theatre I was grateful for that basic experience as it gave me insight into what was needed. My love of theatre opened up a new world for me. I joined a theatre club, The New Lindsey at Notting Hill Gate, where I met interesting people who introduced me to ballet, music concerts and Art galleries. As a child while watching ants, looking for colours in plain brick walls and window-gazing, I'd always known there was a rich world out there somewhere, and now I'd found it. My love of the Arts and sense of adventure within them has never diminished nor has my appreciation of the complexities and simplicities of the natural world failed to excite me. A good book, a painting, a memorable poem, vast oceans of music, mountain, woodlands, a daisy on the lawn, a blade of grass pushing up through concrete, animals. Us. Life itself, with all its conflicts and confusion, is so rich, so magical, I find the only other word I have to describe it is an Americanised word I don't like. *Awesome.*

I left the Day Nursery and took various better-paid child-care and Mother's Help jobs in wealthy homes in Kensington and Hampstead. I lived in, getting my 'keep' plus a small wage. Dad got work with a painting and decorating Firm so things were easier at home and I did not need to contribute. So for the first time I had money to spend. I went to 'C and A' in Kensington High Street and bought a complete new-look style outfit; skirt, coat, hat, gloves, in dark brown, the latest colour. On my day off I went home in all my finery to a welcome of barely-suppressed amusement as I walked from the bus stop past neighbours chatting on the corner and open ridicule from the inevitable gaggle of kids on the doorsteps. Once indoors, despite reassurances from my family that I looked 'lovely' and 'very posh', I didn't leave the house again until after dark, when I had to return to my other world of very different values where I had not looked, nor felt, out of place. I have never bothered with fashion since, always wearing what I like, what I think suits me, and, above all, what I consider appropriate.

Around this time, now more aware of the fight for survival Mum and Dad had always had, I became very idealistic and joined the Young Communist League. I had been to a couple of rallies and been impressed with talk of 'from all according to their abilities, to each according to their needs'. If only! It took me quite a while to realize it doesn't work like that in reality. But I have stayed close to my Socialist roots, only deviating once in later years when Margaret Thatcher came on the political scene. Perhaps now, I though, with a woman in charge we would see some sense and fairness. Wrong again.

Restless, changing jobs fairly frequently, I met up with some very interesting people. Artists in Hampstead, performers, musicians, playwrights, some of whom became well-known. Yehuda Ha-Ezrahi, who wrote the play 'The Cactus Fruit' which was produced in London in the nineteen-fifties. He returned to Israel and became a well-loved writer and a prominent figure in the defence of his country. Bob Monkhouse, the comedian and actor, whose girl-friend rented a room in the house I lived in. Michael Muskett, clarinet player in the Sadler's Wells Orchestra. Michael and I became boy-and-girl-friend for a time. In those days that situation was innocent of all serious commitment and it didn't last. A few, perhaps the most notable being Quentin Crisp and Cal McCord, became long-term personal friends. Many years later they met some of my children and our son Jonathan went on stage with Cal as part of his Cowboy act at the Civic Hall in Grays in Essex. I can still see nine-year old Jonathan's face as he watched his portly mother being picked up in a bear hug and swung around in greeting.

I had known Quentin since I was fifteen, from our New Lindsey and Portobello and Shepherds' Bush Market days, and we remained good friends until he left for his Australia trip. I had been married for some years then and had a bevy of beautiful children, some of whom came to the theatre with me to meet him. We had lunch a few days before, at the Thameside Theatre in Grays, where he was giving his inimitable talk on 'Style'. He told us how scared he was of the Australians and his likely reception by them. Once again I was troubled by the unfairness of prejudice. How can anyone justify rejection of a person or a People based on the colour of their skin, their language, their religion, their culture, or their sexuality? Surely you should get to know them first and then decide whether you liked them or not. And even if you didn't like them surely tolerance was better than instant animosity? To this day one of my favourite words, a word I discovered when I was studying Spanish, is *Convivencia* – learning to live together. Soon after his return he left for America and we never met again. I felt sad the Christmas I heard that he had died. This intelligent, kindly man had been influential in my early teenage years with his quiet acceptance of the complexities, paradoxes, distortions and ironies of life. I always remember him tell me 'Do whatever you want, Darling, - but *Always* do it with *Style!*' I've tried to do that.

Dad became ill and was unable to work. This was a cause of great distress for him. despite the tuberculosis which had affected his spine, deforming a shoulder making him what was loosely termed a 'hunchback', he had always been an excellent, reliable worker and had shown impressive talent in his use of colour with the decorating Firm he worked for. So much so that he was frequently asked for personally when doing jobs for 'the gentry' as he called them: members of the aristocracy and people related to royalty, and celebrities. The contralto Constance Shacklock, Isobel Bailey, the famous soprano, High-ups in the military, with apartments in De Vere Gardens and around Hyde Park. But now he had developed a serious heart condition and could barely walk more than a few steps, stopping to rest against a wall, pretending to look around him. so I took an office job offering good pay and went back home to help Mum. After some rest Dad was able to take a little light part-time job as store-keeper which helped out money-wise and gave Dad back a bit of self-respect.

The office in Holborn distributed typewriter-type in many styles and for many languages. Except for learning about other keyboards, which interested me, I found it deadly dull. The two other girls who worked there had been there for years and were very much a team, making sure I remained an outsider. I was quite happy with that. I didn't actually want to be part of the back-biting conversations about other workers in our office block, or discussion about film stars or hair-dos. They thought I was 'stuck up' and I probably was. The bosses were fine: two middle-aged men and one elderly gentleman who treated us well, with old-fashioned courtesy and respect. Occasionally one of them would take one of us to lunch and birthdays would be acknowledged with a gift and two tickets to a top London show. These lunches, at places like The Waldorf Astoria, The Café Royale, The Dorchester, and front circle tickets to see 'Call Me Madam', 'The King and I', 'South Pacific' opened up a new world for me.

If the weather was reasonably clement I would spend most lunch hours eating my sandwich in the gardens opposite the office. I had a friend, an Israeli writer, Yehuda Ha-Ezrahi, who would sometimes come and keep me company and we would sit and talk theatre and Middle Eastern politics until I had to race against the clock, arriving back breathless and dishevelled to black looks and a wall of disapproval. Many years later, long after we had lost touch, I was to find a book written by Yehuda in a Jerusalem bookshop. It was full of the ideas we had talked about all those lunchtimes ago. Despite the face that he had died some time back it was like meeting up with an old friend. Office lunchtimes, for which we were given luncheon vouchers, were meant to be passed in the little café on the corner of our office block where the other two girls went – together of course. Other than in the gardens my lunchtimes were often spent down the road at the Law Courts, sitting in the public gallery, surreptitiously popping little nibbles of my sandwich into my mouth making sure I was not being observed. Eating in there would certainly have merited disapproval – and, no doubt, removal! The Law Courts fascinated me. How could such seemingly ordinary people have committed such awful crimes? When and why did such thinking come into their heads? I started to try to discover, and if not, to create, their stories. I stayed at that office, working from nine to five and alternate Saturdays, travelling to and from by bus and Tube in the rush hour, for five years, until Dad died when I left to begin nursing. By then I was almost twenty-three. Outside office hours these were my 'hippy' years. Long hair to my waist, long skirts, bare-footed at every opportunity, even in London streets, no make-up, I flouted convention wherever I could get away with it, even to 'skinny-dipping' (in the dark) with mixed groups of friend. Shocking behaviour in my everyday world but quite acceptable among my 'arty' set. Some of my friends spent their holidays in Nudist Camps and thought nothing of it. I, trying to appear more open-minded than I was, at least managed to keep my inner discomfort under wraps. Skinny-dipping and bare feet were the limits of my expression of liberalism much to the amusement of our freedom-loving group.

I had a few months to wait before I could start in the training school so once again I did various part-time jobs, both office and Mother's Help. During this time I took Mum on holiday to the Isle of Wight. It was there I met a man I liked, a farmer. I used to go down at weekends and stay with his sister (we were very proper in those days, the permissive age was yet to come) and we would go sailing, which I loved and I would work on the farm, learning to milk the cows. One of the cows, Mollie, would follow me like a puppy and would have to be shut in when I left, lowing mournfully. Frank always said I had a closer relationship with that cow than I had with him. That was probably true. Frank was the first man with whom I had any romantic involvement, but it didn't develop and when he started to talk of marriage I backed off. I knew I did not want that. The pleasant companionship of a nice, kind, personable young man with a yacht was one thing, the commitment and intimacy of marriage was something else. On my return to London I telephoned and said I would not be going down again. I was going to start nursing.

Nursing was something I had promised myself since those days of evacuation. I had felt safe and cared for in hospital, read all the Sue Barton books, so it seemed a natural outcome that one day I would be a nurse. I applied to my local hospital, St Mary's, and was turned down as I did not have the necessary School Certificate which would have given me entry into further education or a profession. As I was a little older than the usual applicants (normally seventeen and a half to eighteen years) and had left school some eight years previously, they gave me the option of sitting an examination set by them. I agreed to this and passed without difficulty. I was to start as a Probationer in September 1954. But first I had to have a full medical. This threw up another problem: my feet. Seeing the scars I had to explain about the orthopaedic surgery as best I could. It had all been a long time ago and I did not know much detail. The doctor decided that my feet would probably not be up to the demands Nursing would make on them. Seeing my obvious disappointment he asked me what would I do now. I replied I would apply to another hospital – and I would not be so honest next time, I would say the scars were from when I fell off my bike. He smiled and said that in that case they would give me a try. I was in!

My nurse-training years, from 1954 to 1958, have been set apart in my memory. They have a place of their own. Some incidents I can recall with great clarity. One such incident occurred when I handled my first dead body. I had seen my father when he died, touched him, kissed him. I remembered how cold he was, a strange, cold-marble feeling, not like flesh at all. But that was in the funeral parlour down Ladbroke Grove. Apart from that tentative touch and dutiful, expected goodbye kiss I had not needed to handle him at all. But this was different. This was a young patient who had died and I was expected to help prepare her for the mortuary. We had studied the procedure in the training school so I set up the trolley and waited. It was not the first death I had encountered but, other than sitting with distressed relatives, I had had little to do with the previous ones as I was a very junior probationer. So I waited beside the still form in the side-ward bed for somebody more senior to come and take over, mentally checking the equipment on the trolley, wondering what my role would be. Suddenly the Ward Sister appeared at the door. 'Well what are you waiting for? Get on with it Nurse. We haven't got all day.'

'But … but …'

She cast her eye briefly over the trolley.

'That looks OK. You know what to do, don't you?'

'I…I think so … Yes.' You would never admit to a Ward Sister that the Preliminary Training School had not taught you well. That caused problems between the Ward Sisters and the Sister Tutor, who were usually at loggerheads over something, generally on the grounds that those still working on the wards were at the 'rock face' and therefore knew best while the Tutors felt they knew best because of academic achievement. We student nurses pandered to all of them, hoping to keep out of trouble.

'Right. Stop shilly-shallying and get on.'

Yes, I knew what to do. We had practised on a dummy. It couldn't be so different ... could it? Wash hair, wash body along front, wash feet and legs. Turn over and repeat on back. I remember standing for a moment preparing myself mentally then set to work. Taking great care to be gentle and respectful, I approached the body. Remembering about residual fluid from orifices I placed the absorbent packs appropriately then washed and dried her. So far so good. Sister passed by, looked briefly through the window of the cubicle and gave a nod of approval. Apart from a little trembling I had no problem until then. I was half-way through and I was doing all right. I had remembered everything correctly and was feeling more confident. But I did not know about residual air. This had never been mentioned and working on a dummy in the school our Sister Tutor had not thought it necessary to inform us. Or maybe she was so far removed from actual nursing she had forgotten. Whatever the reason I was totally unprepared for what happened next. Turning my patient over, slightly lifting the shoulders to do so, there was a large, hissing escaping breath. I heard myself scream as I turned one way, crashing into the trolley, running for the door, and across the ward, shooting my poor patient off the other side of the bed. Before I reached the large double ward doors a voice stopped me in my tracks.

'Nurse Frost, we do not let our corpses touch the floor! Get back and start again.'

I froze. Sister was coming towards me. Fear of the chaos I was ordered to confront was far outweighed by my fear of the Ward Sister. I began the slow, reluctant return. Water everywhere from the up-turned bowl, scattered packets, instruments, linen, and an uncomplaining, naked patient on the floor between the bedside and the cubicle wall. Where to start? Replace spattered bed-sheet with clean one and pick up patient, placing her very carefully on bed. Would the terrifying experience repeat itself? It did not and I think I gave an audible sigh and relief. Respecting her dignity as though she were still with us I covered her with a towel to await further attention. Cleaning up the cubicle and setting up a fresh trolley was the easy bit. I then returned to my original task, calmer and having learned a thing or two: about the nature of dead bodies, about the limitations of book-learning compared with the power of experience – and about myself. When I had finished, just a curt nod from Sister showed that all was well this time. The incident was never openly referred to again but I suspect it is still whispered about as a warning to young trainee nurses.

I enjoyed my training. St Mary's was, and is, a large general Teaching Hospital with two subsidiary Children's hospitals, Paddington Green and Princess Louise, nearby. The first six weeks for all new students were spent in the Preliminary Training School with no contact with real patients. In fact we only visited the hospitals once, when we were shown around the wards. After an exam to show we had mastered the basics we were allowed on to the Wards and straightaway entered onto the rota to put in a full working week. For all future study we were supposedly released to attend day or half-day lectures, but these study sessions often overlapped with what should have been our normal off-duty. The lectures were important, and Sister Tutor tyrannical, so of course we attended. The work was hard, the hours long and poorly paid. There was no such thing as overtime. We got a basic monthly pay, irrespective of hours served. You worked on until your tasks were completed.

If you were slow, or delayed, this encroached on your scheduled off-duty. You got off when you were given permission to go. Sometimes, if you were on a split-duty (8am-8pm with 3 hours off from 2-5) it could be hardly worth-while going back to the Nurse's home so we would sit and rest, read the paper or gossip in the day room or Doctors' sitting room.

Although we did such a responsible job, in our off-duty we were treated like children. If we had an evening off we had to be in by 10.30p.m. unless we had previously applied for, and been granted, a late pass by Matron. She would want to know where we were going, who with, and at what time the event was expected to finish. I look back with admiration on our inventiveness, our ability to create very credible stories delivered with straight-forward, look-me-in-the-eye innocence. Did she know we were running rings around her? Probably. After all, she had been a junior nurse herself once. For those who had to keep to the 10.30 rule, which was most of us on most nights, we had our ways of by-passing the system. At 10.30p.m. precisely, Home Sister, in charge of the Nurses' Home and its residents would go along to the door at the end of the corridor and bolt it firmly, one at the top and a bigger one at the bottom. She would then check the bathrooms and put out the corridor lights except for one small glow for authorised latecomers, and go to bed. Those with late passes had to come in through the hospital main entrance and check in at the night porter's lodge. No chance of slipping in unseen. We in our rooms were allowed to stay up and keep our lights on as long as we kept the radio and our voices low. Soon after we heard the click of Home Sister's door closing, one of us would creep along to gently slide back the bolts, which we kept well-vaselined, to facilitate entry for the stop-outs. That was the easy bit. The difficulty was that whoever was on let-in details had also to be up at least an hour before Home Sister – who was an early riser – to replace the bolts. And there was always the risk that someone might be ill during the night and need medical care. That did happen once when one of the girls developed appendicitis and had to be rushed to theatre. One of the girls slipped the bots back into place, hoping that no-one had noticed and two poor miscreants spent the rest of the night hunched against the door at the top of the fire escape awaiting discovery when Home Sister re-opened at 6.30a.m. One can only guess at the wrath poured upon them in the privacy of Matron's office. The girls, feeling they'd been betrayed, didn't want to talk about it but for a long time afterward they were very subdued, both on and off duty and developed an unreasonable antipathy to the poor appendectomy patient. As did Home Sister who muttered and complained about the stupidity of the young. Why on earth hadn't the girl had the sense to report sick during civilized daytime hours? The rest of us were just thankful that thanks to someone's quick thinking she had no idea of our nightly deceptions. She prided herself on running 'a tight ship' and we were happy that she should continue to believe it.

In those days food for patients and staff was cooked in the hospital kitchens, not sent in as it mostly is now. One of our cooks was quite a character, regaling us with stories about a young crow she had rescued when it had fallen from its nest. This bird, name Baby Bird now lived with her and her husband in a top-floor flat in Shepherd's Bush and had apparently taken over their lives. It ate from their plates, scattering food across the table, played in the sink splashing water everywhere and generally made a nuisance of itself whenever anybody called. Also it had learned to talk: a stream of invective, to her shame and the amusement of her husband, no doubt the originator of its limited but colourful vocabulary. Apparently a local vicar, having trailed up three flights of stairs, was greeted with a tirade of unintelligible abuse punctuated by very clear obscenities.

After the first few weeks of the bird's residence they regretted taking it in and left the kitchen window open in the hope that it would fly away but it obviously knew where it was well off. As their increasingly recalcitrant resident became even more dominant its reluctant hosts searched for a solution to their problem. They pestered the local library for books on birds, wrote to the newspapers, talked about it to anyone who would listen. There were lots of suggestions, none of which worked. The main one, which undoubtedly would have been successful, was to have it put down. This they could not bear to do. They acquired a cat thinking that would put the bird in its place. Baby Bird was said to have terrorised the poor creature, screaming at it and attacking it until it turned tail and fled as though its fur were on fire. They never saw it again.

One ruse, suggested by one of our doctors, looked hopeful. He said they should take the bird in a covered cage, so that it couldn't see where it was going, drive as far as they could into the countryside, release it near woodland, then drive home hell for leather. This, early one Sunday morning, they did, arriving back in Shepherd's Bush only to find Baby sitting at the top of the steps, exhausted and complaining bitterly. I was not sure I believed all this, although Vera did not seem the sort to be given to flights of fancy, so, on the pretext of being particularly interested in birds in captivity, I wangled an invitation to go and see for myself. When I arrived Baby was taking a bath in the washing-up bowl, splashing and jumping in and out on to the draining-board. Seeing me he shrieked alarmingly and swooped at me, knocking off my glasses. Vera, trying to catch him, chased him with a towel in her hands. Round and round the tiny kitchen they went, into the living-room, Baby all the time flapping his dripping wings furiously and using, loudly and unmistakedly, the most atrocious language. All attempts at re-capturing Baby having failed Vera gave up and sat heavily on a chair, the towel across her knees. She couldn't even offer me a cup of tea, she said, not while that Devil's creature was in this mood. Devil's creature indeed, you could almost believe it. I'd seen enough to convince me that Vera was no fantasist. Vera left the hospital soon after so I never found out what happened to Baby. I've always felt Angela Carter could have made a good story out of it.

When I went home on my day off during the time that Vera was with us I would recount the latest 'Baby' episode to Mum who was fascinated. She loved anything to do with birds, even Uncle Charlie's pigeons, which Auntie Rose couldn't stand. She couldn't understand why Vera would want to get rid of such a remarkable bird and thought that a little inconvenience was a small price to pay for the experience. I said that I would take her over to Shepherd's Bush sometime to see for herself, but, regrettably, somehow I never did.

My nursing years, generally speaking, were happy ones. In the P.T.S. I'd made good friends, a Scottish girl, Mary, a German girl, Ludmilla and Rosemary, who is still my friend today. Our disciplines, Rosemary in General and Mary, Ludmilla and I in Paediatrics, placed us in different hospitals much of the time but Rosie and I met up whenever we could. Rosie and I had had completely different upbringings and perhaps because of this I think we were good for each other. Watching her gentleness, experiencing her kindness and consideration of others, I learned you didn't have to be strong, on the defensive all the time, that you could let your guard down. And she liked eating cockles and whelks at a market stall, eating chips out of the paper, talking about everything and anything without it having to be approved of. Being friends taught us a lot about people and about ourselves. She and her sisters had been educated at Cheltenham Ladies College, her father had been a surgeon at St Mary's and was now a G.P. Rosie's family was wonderful to me whenever I went down to stay with them at their house in Cowfold in Sussex. Instead of looking down on me, with my city-slum background and rough and tough street wisdom as well they might have done, they liked me. When we, together with her sister Jill, decided to go on holiday together, they encouraged and helped facilitate it, saying they felt I would help keep their daughters sensible and safe. I was, of course, a couple of years older which may have helped.

The first holiday Rosie, Jill and I took together was to Holland. It was the nearest, it was flat – and we had bikes. I got my first passport, the others already had theirs from previous holidays abroad. We each packed a hold-all, strapped it to the carrier of our bicycles, made sure we each had a pump and a puncture outfit, and set off for Harwich.

Until we boarded the ferry my experience of the sea had been a day trip to Southend on bank holiday Monday with Mum and Dad and more recently, a train trip to Brighton with friends from the hospital, and sailing in the Solent. While I was growing up, even after the War, August Bank Holiday was special. Families all around us had booked places on coaches – we called them charabancs in those days – to take us to the seaside. For working men the outing was often arranged by their Firms. For most of us it was the only holiday of the year.

One day in which to leave the smoke and grime of London behind. It was always a very jolly occasion. People dressed in their 'Sunday best', laughing, joking with each other, excited children, some with little buckets and spades, others clutching cocoa tins and old wooden spoons, dreaming about sand castles, squabbling over window seats, tension building up as we waited for the driver. Then the drive through our familiar streets, through East London into the suburbs of Essex and on past Essex towns, Brentford, Romford, Benfleet, Rayleigh and Southend-on-sea.

Southend, with the wonderfully lit-up, dome-topped Kursaal which held the circus and the Fair, and the games arcade; its cockle and whelk stalls, its sparkling sea and sandy beach. And its pier. The longest pier in the world we were told. Whether it was or not I didn't know. It didn't matter, it was glorious. Once we went on the little train right to the end of it, seeing the rolling sea beneath us through the gaps in the track. Heady, scary, exciting stuff. Mum lost her hat in the wind at the end of the pier, a little black hat with a feather and a tiny veil. Mum grumbled as we watched it bobbing away far below, looking like a lonely black duck as it floated away.

Down on the beach we paddled, made sand castles which were jumped on by the other kids so we jumped on theirs. Scraps erupted which were soon sorted out by the adults, dragged away from reading their newspapers.

Back on the charabanc everyone agreed a good day had been had by all. We children clutched our winnings from the Fair: a toy, a goldfish in a jam-jar. We held on to our bags of coins from the one-armed bandits or bemoaned our luck, sure that the machines had been rigged to rob us of our pennies and halfpennies. Winners or losers we were all sleepy, grimy, sandy and happy. The adults, too, seemed content. They talked and laughed and before we were out of Southend on the road home, had broken into song. Most of the songs everybody knew. 'Tipperary', 'My old man said follow the van', 'Roll out the Barrel', 'Show me the way to go home', 'Who were you with last night?' 'In the shade of the old apple tree'. Here and there someone would start up one we couldn't sing along to, and we'd listen to a lone voice singing a mournful Irish one about longing and loss like 'The Mountains of Mourne' or 'I will take you home again Kathleen'. But maudlin mood could not be allowed to take over and this would soon be followed by something lively like 'Hands, Knees and Boomps-a-Daisy' during which several people would get up into the aisle and start bumping bottoms, falling, squealing, into the laps of those still seated as the coach lurched. Nearing London we would start to spot landmarks and the men would wonder aloud if we would be back before the pubs closed. Arguments would break out then, the women saying they had to get these kids home to bed and asking the men where they had kept the money for booze. 'If I'd know you had any money left we could have …' etc. But I don't remember the arguments ever coming to anything, unlike the arguments on Friday and Saturday nights when the pubs closed. Nobody would allow this day to be spoilt.

As I stood at the rail of the ferry taking us over to The Hook of Holland, just a name and a dot on the map, I don't know what I expected. This vast expanse of rolling sea was nothing like Southend or The Solent, that was for sure. I suppose what I was feeling was awe. I had experienced awe before, many times. Sunsets, storms, the complexity of the human body, the study of the worlds within worlds through the microscope. So much to wonder at. But this was so *close*. I could almost touch it. I felt the power of it, tossing what had seemed our enormous Ferry about like a cork. They said it was a rough crossing and Rosie and Jill stayed below for most of it, feeling queasy, but I loved it and did not feel the least bit sea-sick. Arriving in Holland we were instantly made aware of the importance of bicycles. It seemed almost everyone used them. There were cars of course, and lorries and giant container-lorries, but these were chiefly for carrying goods. For people to get about generally, from the eldest to the youngest, the bicycle was obviously the optimum form of transport. We could hardly believe our eyes as we saw a whole family pass on two bikes: father with one small boy on the cross-bar, a large box of shopping on the carrier at the back with another child perched on the top, legs outstretched on either side. Alongside him the mother with a toddler in a seat on the carrier and a baby in the basket on the front. As we found our way on to the cycle path running alongside the Autobahn we saw very little children probably no older than three or four years, riding big adult bicycles, standing up to reach the pedals, and there were the elderly: women in long skirts and aprons, men wearing caps, smoking pipes and carrying large boxes of flowers, cheeses or vegetables. Most of the bikes around us were large and heavy with no gears and no lights. We felt like amateurs with our smart, gear-assisted, legally-lit machines.

We cycled all around Holland, up the west side, across the nineteen-mile long Afslutdijk with the North Sea on one side and the Zeider Zee, now turned into a freshwater lake, on the other and down through Friezland to the Belgium border. Halfway across the Afslutdijk there was an Observation Tower. We were shocked to see how close the vast, threatening North Sea came to the top of the dyke. It seemed the whole road and possibly the whole of Holland could be totally submerged in moments. Coming down from the Tower, without a word to each other, we got on our bikes and pedalled furiously in a hurry to reach the comparative safety of the other side.

We stayed at Youth Hostels, all of them clean, friendly and some, especially the one just before our venture on the Afslutdijk, even luxurious. However we did rough it just a bit.

One night, after a wonderful day at the Cheese Market in Haarlem followed by a series of mini-disasters; punctures, getting lost etc. we arrived too late to book in at the hostel so we set about looking for somewhere to spend the night. We had no money for bed and breakfast or accommodation other than the minimal Youth Hostel charge so we went outside the town. On a nearby farm we found an empty barn and settled in there, hoping to be up and away next morning before we were discovered. But we were very tired and the barn, with plenty of hay bales, smelled sweet and looked quite comfortable. Luckily we had bought a round, red-waxed cheese from the market and had some water left in the bottles hanging on our bikes so we were able to make a meagre supper before settling down for the night. We were woken from a sound sleep by the shaft of daylight as a man stood in the doorway. Fortunately for us he spoke some English and was amused, saying we looked like startled rabbits. He took us to the house where we were given the opportunity to tidy ourselves up and were given a good breakfast of ham, cheese, bread, butter and coloured sugar crystals. His wife was delighted to have visitors from England and wanted us to sing English hymns for them. We obliged with a few of the well-known ones. Although I had been in the choir at school my hymns were mostly in Latin so Rosie and Jill had a better repertoire than I had but at least I could join in 'The Lord is my Shepherd' which was their favourite. These hospitable people were so friendly and had made us so welcome we were sorry to leave them. They came on to the road and waved us off as we pedalled away. Everywhere we went going up this west side of Holland towards the Afslutdijk we received a warm and friendly reception. Even the Police, with whom we came in contact a few times, were tolerant and helpful. Our first two encounters were accidental due to us being English, ignorant and (mainly me) thinking we knew it all. The first time was in The Hague soon after we arrived. We had to cross the city centre to get to the Autobahn leading northwards. There appeared to be a very circuitous route for bicycles bypassing the massive conglomeration of traffic. We thought we could just cut across. Oh, no we couldn't! As we started to nose our way across in front of a large lorry that had stopped at the lights we were startled by loud blasts on whistles, shouting and suddenly we were surrounded by Police on motorbikes. 'Afstigen! Eruit gaan!' they were yelling at us, signalling for us to get off, manoeuvring us back to the side of the road. We didn't understand the language but they were very clear about what they wanted us to do. At the police station we were given refreshments while we waited for a policeman who spoke English, to come and give us a lecture on how to use the roads in Holland. A week or so later, coming down the Friesland side, we did the same thing again, but in full knowledge this time, 'accidentally' straying on to the Autobahn. The result was much the same and the refreshments more than welcome as we were almost broke. I have often wondered since if the Police there ever go together and what they would have thought of three young English girls taking *them* for a ride. Apart from a kindly lorry driver that was the only warmth or friendliness we encountered in our ride through Friesland.

Thankfully we had crossed the Afslutdijk without drowning and we were ready to pass through Dutch towns and villages, meeting with the people again. Life appeared to be very different here. People, including little children, working in the fields, in traditional dress looking like something out of an Old Masters painting. Horses and carts on the road along with the inevitable bicycles carrying whole families also in traditional dress. Old people on long expanses of road walking considerable distances, wearing clogs and carrying enormous baskets. Life was obviously harder here. Reaching our first village we tried to ask directions to the Youth Hostel. We were met with a blank stare. No English? We would try again. There was a little shop which looked like a café as well. Perhaps they would help us. As we entered we were signally to stop. The young woman pointed to the door and shook her head. 'No! Out!' We did not know what we had done wrong but it was plain she was not going to serve us. We left, puzzled and upset. On the road again we received shouts and jeers, children spat as we passed. Later we were told that they hated the English. This was in 1954 – probably too soon after the War when antagonisms still ran deep. Many people on this side had been pro-German. Also another thing that put us right out of favour, especially in the North, was we were wearing shorts. I suppose among people all around us covered from head to foot, including bonnets or caps, we, with our bare heads and especially our bare legs presented quite a challenge.

We were glad when a lorry-driver stopped and offered us a lift, which we were happy to accept. He dropped us further South where the ambience was once again tolerant, warm and friendly. On our way back to the return Ferry we nearly missed the boat as my old Hercules bike, which had only one gear, decided it had had enough and seized up. Standing on the pedals and grinding away I thought I wouldn't make it but a man came alongside and, putting his hand in my back, pushed me along until we reached the gangplank. Needless to say, on arrival back at Harwich, we completed our journey back to London by train.

Rosie and I took a couple of other holidays together. We went to Austria and North Wales – but not on our bikes!

I was always concerned when I was away as I didn't like leaving Mum. Her health was always a worry. We didn't have a phone so I couldn't check if she was alright. I always brought little gifts back for her and told her all about the holiday – well, perhaps not all – which she enjoyed, but I know she didn't like me going. She loved it when I took her on holiday on our own and would talk about it for ages afterwards making me feel as if I'd done something special. She was on her own after Dad died and she met and married George Baker, and she was lonely. And she was my Mum. What else would I do? During work time it was easy to keep an eye on her; the hospital was nearby and it didn't take long for me to pop home when I had a couple of hours off-duty. She liked that. We would have a cup of tea and sometimes I would 'do' her feet for her, bathing them in scented water, trimming the nails and massaging them with cream. She had corns and callouses from her early years wearing ill-fitting shoes and a foot pampering session was something she loved. If she was going out that evening I would wash and set her hair. We had no bathroom so it was a bit of a performance for her to wash her hair on her own as she had to stand on a box Dad had made her to be able to lean over the sink.

During my last year of training I was allowed to 'live out' so left the Nurses Home and moved back in with Mum. This was before she had decided to marry her companion, George Baker, and while I was trying to decide what I wanted to do when I had qualified. That's when fate stepped in and took over. I think it was John Lennon who once said 'Life is something that happens while you're making other plans.'

My sister and her husband Ronnie lived a few doors away from a family from Gibraltar who, despite their obviously very Spanish lifestyle and speaking hardly any English, were, they informed us with real patriotic pride, not Spanish, but British. Pam became very friendly with them and helped them with their English so when one of the younger members of the family came over to visit them it was arranged for him to give Pam some lessons in Spanish in exchange. He called at Pam's flat. She was out. I, with a couple of hours off-duty popped round to see her at the same time. We met on the stairs leading up to her flat and sat talking, then went our separate ways, he, after a brief stay, back to Gibraltar and I back to the hospital to ponder my future. Eighteen months later we met again, when he called at Mum's flat in Powis Square looking for me. Apparently he hadn't been able to get me out of his head and I, too, had been preoccupied and puzzled by the intensity of feeling I had for someone I hardly knew. I even toyed with the idea of going to Gibraltar to see if we could meet. I knew it was a very small place and there would be a good chance of doing so. Had I fallen in love? I didn't know for sure until he came back. That was in April 1958, just before I took my Finals.

Having qualified I left the hospital and took a post as Deputy Matron at the Day Nursery, where I had started work at fifteen, while I awaited the result of my enquiries into refugee work in the Middle East. I also worked part-time at a Social Centre in Ladbroke Grove. This had been set up to help immigrants, chiefly from the Caribbean following the arrival of the 'Windrush' in 1948 and subsequent sailings, who were having difficulties settling. Of course they were. Prejudice was rife. Work was no problem – we needed their manpower, but their request for accommodation was all too frequently met with a door closed in the face. Specific notices, 'No Blacks' were everywhere. Once again I was troubled by the unfairness of it all and the ugliness of prejudice. Perhaps, in some small way, I could help.

Then José Luis Fiol, anglicised as Joseph Fiol, Pepe to the family, arrived on my doorstep and all future plans disappeared into oblivious to be replaced by other hopes, other dreams, as yet undreamed of.

We were married on the second of August that same year. And there begins the story which continues today, fifty-four years later on. Our wedding at St. Francis of Assisi, Pottery Lane, the Church in which I had been baptised, was simple. I had sat up the night before finishing the three-quarter length broderie anglaise dress I had made myself with the help of the lady in the flat above. I carried a small bouquet of yellow tea-roses and lilies-of-the-valley. Pam bought us a wedding cake which she had ordered from Whiteley's in Queensway. After the ceremony – a full hour-long Nuptial Mass as we were both, at that time Catholics, we all, friends and family, went back to Mum's flat for a buffet which Mum, Pam and I had laid out before we left. An ex-neighbour of ours, Bert Hall (yes, he and his son really were named Albert Hall!) played our old piano for us. We left them, still singing, to spend a few days honeymoon in, of all things, an old varda parked at the bottom of an extensive garden in Oxfordshire. We couldn't afford a proper holiday but saw this advertised in the evening paper. It was cheap and, we thought, would be romantic. Romantic it wasn't! With every movement it clattered, banged, creaked and squeaked. At night just turning over in the narrow bed caused such a rocking and a clamouring that we suffered agonies of cramp and pins-and-needles before attempting any change of position. And the day-time, if anything, was worse as there were often people about in the surrounding gardens. We spent most of our time walking in the countryside and visiting Oxford University and Aylesbury Market. We could not wait to go home and did so three days sooner than we needed to. Enough was enough. As a memento we took back a little porcelain duck with a chipped foot, which we saw in the window of the gift-shop in Aylesbury. The shop assistant didn't want to sell us a damaged item and offered to find us a perfect, boxed one but for some reason we insisted it had to be *that* one. We still have it on our mantelpiece.

Mum, by this time, had married George Baker so Pepe and I moved to Leicester and set up home with his parents and brother, near to where his sister Lourdes and her husband lived. A year later, after the loss of our first baby, we moved to a flat of our own where we had Jonathan. We had no money so moved everything we possessed bit by bit using an old enormous grey bassinet pram which we borrowed. By the end of the day we were both exhausted. Late evening saw me, clutching the last of our treasures, gratefully being pushed in the pram to our new home. Our new neighbours probably thought we were drunk, turning up as we did looking the worse for wear, the pram squeaking and creaking grumpily, and we two giggling uncontrollably at the bizarreness of it all.

Our two rooms and a box-room with a Baby Belling cooker were at the top of the three-storey house. We had no running water or toilet and had to go down two flights of stairs to use these facilities. Although this was fine for us at the beginning it was obviously unsuitable for the baby we were soon expecting. Our landlord, who was very impressed by the way we had brightened up the flat: it was amazing the effect burnt-orange and lime wallpaper could have on otherwise gloomy rooms, was concerned for us but hadn't got any other property available. So, incredible as it still seems today, he bought a little terraced house nearby, lent us the deposit, and arranged the mortgage on it for us. He also gave us his own lovely Victorian Christening gown for the baby. It was, he said, his sadness that he would never have need of it.

The next couple of years passed very quickly. We had both Jonathan and Sarah while living in our little house in Fairfield Street. We thought we were settled but Life had other plans for us. Pepe still had his dreams of being an artist so took jobs which, while earning money to support his family, allowed him the freedom to have time in the day to draw and paint, and perhaps even to go to Art College. There was little work at the shoe-factory where he was working when we married so he left there to look for better, steadier employment. For a time he was a night-cleaner on the buses, then he was a postman. He applied to the local Art College to study for the Art Foundation Course. That was unheard of. A married man with two children, and the commitment of a mortgage! Mature students were a rarity in thos days, not a norm as they are now. Unsurprisingly, although recognising his talent, Leicester Art College would not offer him a place, so it was either give up or move on. So we left our little house, passing on the mortgage and all our furniture to his sister, Lourdes, and moved into a caravan parked on a site near the next Art College, Loughborough, where he applied for, and was offered a place, complete with a Grant, which we lived off for the next three-and-a-half years. Any gaps in my management of hand-to-mouth existence still left over from my childhood were filled in during those years. I'm still inclined to pick off nettle tops, gather sorrel, wild garlic and dandelion leaves to add to soups and salads and I still can't tolerate waste. After playing at Gypsies in the caravan for a few months, facing a daily battle with mud and invading armies of earwigs, we found a house for rent in Mountsorrel, about six miles from the College. We moved in and our third child, Victoria, was born there.

It was there I learned a very important lesson: never take your eyes off a helpful three-year-old. Jonathan, my 'big boy', elder brother to Sarah, aged fifteen months and Victoria, just a few weeks, loved to help his mummy. That was fine when we were all together and I was supervising but occasionally he would think of something which would prove to be far from helpful, like when he put the last clean nappies in the sink with the washing-up (before the days of disposables) and picked me a bunch of flowers from the display in the greengrocers while I was selecting vegetables. One such well-meaning effort had such impact it still makes me go cold to think of it, and what might have been. I was feeding Victoria when a neighbour came in through the back door, looking worried.

'Have you seen what your Jonty is doing?'

'He's OK. He's playing on the front. The gate is fixed – he can't get out.'

Now the front of our rented house was set to lawn, a very neat, lush pocket-handkerchief square of green, a safe place for him to play where I could keep an eye on him through the window. But I was feeding the baby, singing to her and my other little one. My mind was not on my busy eldest child.

'I think you'd better come and see'. Putting the baby in her crib, unhooking Sarah, as usual glued to my leg, I got up and went towards the door, meeting Jonathan on his way in. he was proudly carrying a can of creosote, almost too heavy for him.

'I did water the garden for you, Mummy.'

Oh, he had. He had. I'll never forget the sight of that creosoted lawn, nor the emotions which coursed through me. Shock. And fear. What would we say to the Landlord? We had no money – we were living on a grant so could not offer to repair the damage. Would we be thrown out? Where would we go? And Pepe? What would he say? Surely he would be angry that I'd let him do it. What was I thinking of? What if the creosote had burned him, or was toxic. Oh God, what if our little boy had come to harm? Jonathan was still standing beside me, waiting to be praised. I grabbed the can, which had been left by the workmen putting up fencing at the back. I don't remember what I said. I checked his hands and his mouth. He seemed to be alright, just puzzled, then cross when I made him come inside.

'What will you do?' my neighbour asked.

What would I do? I had no idea. I thought perhaps I should contact the agent we rented the house from, throw myself on his mercy. We didn't have a phone so it would mean making an appointment, and anyway I thought I should speak to Pepe first.

Seeing my distress my neighbour looked thoughtful.

'Leave it with me' she said, and left.

It was dark when Pepe came home and the children were in bed. I told him of the day's happenings, castigating myself so he didn't have to. He didn't say much, just was more worried than usual. Next morning, early, we went out to view the damage. What creosoted lawn? Where was the large, ugly brown patch? There was a green lawn. True, there were cracks between the turves, but a green lawn none the less.

Joan had said leave it with her. Perhaps her two boys, Michael and Terry, had had a hand in this? But how? Feeling great relief on the one hand and a complete puzzlement on the other I went in to see to the children and Pepe went off to college. We'd have to look into it later.

Pushing the pram with the two babies, Jonathan toddling beside, I became aware of something different in the surroundings. The long road to the shops had deep grass verges which now displayed, at irregular intervals, large brown patches of soil. Coupled with my knowledge of Joan's wild teenagers who, she always said, would be the death of her, the explanation for my instant lawn became apparent. For a long time afterwards I was afraid to go out, not wanting to see the accusing spaces and afraid to stay in in case righteous indignation telling everybody 'I did water the garden and Mummy was *cross*.' I wonder if that was to blame for his later objection to helping me in the garden. He always had to be well bribed to do a bit of weeding and even after a price above a justified amount had been negotiated he would still have an air of grievance.

From Leicestershire we moved to South Wales where Pepe had a place at Newport College of Art.

Wales. Where, for the first time I was alone with my husband and little family. In London we had had both Pepe's and my family around us, in Leicester Pepe's family had predominated although we saw my mother, until she died, and my sister and her children, quite frequently. But here, in what was to all intents and purposes a foreign country we were on our own. A little townie family uprooted and transplanted into the heart of the Welsh countryside. On receiving Pepe's letter of acceptance on the Dip. AD.Course we had advertised for accommodation in the South Wales newspaper: 'Art student, wife, three small children and 'bump' require rented accommodation while studying at Newport College of Art.' We had hoped, indeed expected, that we would be able to rent a little house somewhere near to the College. Not so. The only reply we received was from a couple who had recently bought a large, 12-roomed Rectory in Wolvesnewton, some eleven miles away from Newport, who had rooms to spare and were willing to offer us a couple of bedrooms, kitchen and living room in exchange for a very reasonable rent. So, one day in August 1963 we set out for the Welsh hills feeling a bit like pioneers heading for the Wild West.

The owners, Kit and Jeanne Hopkins, had only met Pepe on one occasion when he had gone to visit the College and had gone (walking all the way from Newport to Wolvesnewton) to introduce himself to them. A sort of mutual interview to find out if the situation would be child-friendly – and if the owners would accept us in their home. On his return Pepe said the only question he was asked was, not if we were married or would we be able to pay the rent, but did we use a fireguard! They had two small children and were obviously safety-conscious. Undoubtedly our sort of people. Yes, we would go there.

Our arrival was bizarre to say the least. We had travelled from Leicester in Michael and Terry's van: Pepe, pregnant me, a three-year-old, a two-year-old, a one-year-old and a pram loaded up with all our worldly goods plus a couple of tea chests on which we sat in the back. We arrived at The Old Rectory in the early afternoon to find no-one there. The owners, were away but had left a note telling us where to find the key and instructing us to make ourselves at home. What trust!

When they returned a week later we were able to confirm what remarkable people they were, for not only had they turned their home over to complete strangers but they became, and have remained, close and devoted friends ever since. Kit, sadly, died recently but Jeanne is still my dearest friend.

There are many memorable highlights from our time in Wales, each a story in itself. There were Pepe's battles to get to and from College involving an almost personal war with a moped scooter resulting in a reluctant move to a rented house in Malpas to be nearer the College. There was the joy and excitement of the birth of three more children, Claire while we were still at Wolvesnewton and Caroline and Virginia before we left Wales for Essex. During this time we made more wonderful friends, Roger from College, who, towards the end of the Course came to live with us and became a lifelong friend and is still considered a part of our family. Elizabeth, my Health Visitor, who brought her daughter Mary to be looked after when she was working. Gloria, whose daughter Josie was 'best friends' with our little Sarah. Mr Thomas, the policeman whose son Peter and our Jonathan were always together, in and out of school. It felt as though both families had two boys. While four-year-old Sarah would often be playing with Josie at Gloria's house next to the woods and Jonathan would be either at Peter's or at school, three-year-old Mary, the same age as Victoria, would be with me and the younger children 'helping' me. With a fifteen-month-old and a new baby (Caroline) that help could make a ten-minute-job last two hours! Sometimes, when the weather was good, I would collect all the children together, put the babies in the pram packed in with packets of sandwiches and bottles of water, milk feeds, spoons and nappies, reins to control a toddler with a strong urge to wander once her feet contacted the ground, and a good plastic bag to hold all the inevitable wet and dirty nappies, sicked-on tops and other accumulated debris, and off we would go to the park. There we would take over the roofed wooden shelter which would become our house, a ship at sea, a cave, a mud hut on a desert island, a shop and, once (Jonathan's suggestion) an igloo. The fact that on that occasion the weather turned first misty then wet and cold helped the game along until it got too bad and we went home.

Several times in the holidays Elizabeth came to take us to Barry Island, a rare treat for us. Although we were not far away, I could not get there by public transport with the children without tremendous difficulty. I tried it once just before we had Caroline. With my four I packed up the pram and walked the several miles from Malpas to Newport railway station, got on the train for Cardiff in the guard's van, changed at Cardiff for the train to Barry, accepting kindly help with the pram up and down steps and clinging on to my toddler Victoria (on reins) protesting all the way that she was 'too big to play horses'.

Finally arriving at Barry Island, gratefully I sat down on a rock to feed the baby, keeping my eye on the girls who were making sandcastles. Jonathan said he would collect shells for them. I was tired after all the effort of getting there and relaxed for a moment. Claire was fed, changed and happy, the girls were having a lovely time – but where was Jonathan? I don't think I have ever felt such panic before or since. I could not leave the others to go and look for him, so gathered the children, putting the little one in the pram, and, leaving everything else in a pile. I discovered how difficult it is to wheel a pram on sand. Luckily several people had noticed a small boy wandering about and pointed me in the direction of the Coastguard's hut. There he was, my treasured boy, not drowned or taken away or being involved in a hundred dreadful scenarios as I had pictured during my search, but drinking orange juice and eating cake. I was so relieved I did not know whether to laugh or cry, hug him or scold him. He solved the problem by telling me firmly 'I didn't do anything naughty Mummy. I didn't go too near the water like you told me but I did getted lost. So I asked a man where do the lost boys go and he fetched me here. And I've got cake.' The next time we went to the seaside we went in Elizabeth's car. Elizabeth, slim and slight, a portly and pregnant me, Mary, Jonathan, Sarah, Victoria, Claire, and the dog. Plus all the necessary paraphernalia for a day out with small children. The next time anyone tells me they could get sixteen people in a mini I will believe them. (Before the days of compulsory seat belts, of course).

Around this time we had two brief visits from Pam, one when she came down to stay for a few days while we were still at Jeanne and Kit's and the other later, when we had moved to Malpas, when she brought her three children, small boys plus two foster children, a girl Diane, who was ten and a boy of eight, to stay with us while she had extensive hospital treatment. For a couple of weeks, with nine young children to care for, seven of them under six, our home resembled not so much a crèche as a bear garden. Young Diane was a treasure and loved to help with the babies but two of Pam's boys were hard work, fighting a lot and creating mayhem just for the fun of it. Of course they missed their Mum and Dad and our life was all very strange to them so it was difficult for us all. Keeping the children fed and safe while trying to keep some kind of order became a priority. At the end of each day, if the kids were tucked up in bed and the house was still standing we felt we'd done well. Of course there were still the broken nights to get through; feeds, wee-wees, drinks, bad dreams and numerous other ruses to get us to a bedside. As we hadn't enough beds for them all the children slept 'top-and-tail' with a pillow at each end of the bed, so one wakeful one would disturb the other and there were squabbles over feet poking into faces. Although willing to help we were not sorry when Ronnie and a recovered Pam came and collected their brood. Somehow we summoned up enough energy to give them a hearty 'Goodbye' wave. We saw very little of them after that as a couple of years later they emigrated to South Africa. We kept in touch by telephone and letter until Pam's death at sixty-five. We are still in touch with the boys and their families. Nigel, his wife Avril and lovely little daughter Tamia have been over to visit us in recent years. After her death they honoured Pam's wish to be brought back home, bringing her ashes back to be scattered at a British sea-side. We chose Brighton, a favourite place for us all when we were young.

Jonathan, much to his delight, started school, a small friendly village school just around the corner. Remembering my own experience I was apprehensive, taking him in on his first day but I didn't need to worry. He loved it and went off happily each day, meeting his best friend Peter Thomas at the gate so they could go in together. After school he would either go to play at Peter's house or Peter would come to us and on Saturday afternoons Peter's father, would take the boys to watch the football.

One day during Jonathan's first weeks at school sticks in my mind. His teacher, Mrs Leigh, came to the house during lunchtime. Seeing her at the door I felt a moment of panic. Jonathan! But then I realized she was smiling and saying she hoped I didn't mind her 'popping-in' but she just had to share something with me. She was giggling so it couldn't be bad. It turned out that our little boy was a bit of a puzzle to them. They couldn't decide whether he was completely innocent or was 'sending them up'. I said he did have a wicked sense of humour so I would hazard a guess at the latter option. Apparently the children were learning to write numbers and Jonathan was getting some of his facing the wrong way. Mr Dovey, the Headmaster, told him that if, by the end of the morning, he could produce a whole page of numbers all the right way round he would take him to the village shop and buy him an ice-cream. With head down, tongue slightly protruding and a frown of concentration Jonathan tackled his task. At the end of the session he proudly produced the result. A whole page, cram-full from top to bottom, with the figure *one*, 1111111111111111111111111111...

All the right way round, he pointed out proudly. He got his ice-cream.

Remembering, I wonder, where did he go, our lovely, bright, shining, happy boy? How did he get lost in the maze of the dreadful mental illness that, in later years, was to claim his life? An illness that claimed the lives of Pepe's brother Mario, other members of the Fiol family and one which Pepe has battled – and still battles – all his adult life. To what sunless, joyless, demon-inhabited shores do they travel, some never to return? And, once having confronted their dragons, do they pass through the Badlands? To what?

Where do they go, those who die but who we feel are still with us? Where are they other than in our memory? Religions give us their unverified answers, wishes on which to pin to our dream of immortality, our hopes of future life. But I do not believe in Heaven or Hell. But I do believe in immortality and continuity through change. I think that nothing which has been brought into existence can be uncreated. It is. Therefore it is forever. But not necessarily in the same form. Given time, trees become coal become diamonds. And all comes from Stardust and will return to Stardust. But after Stardust? Therein lies the Mystery. So we still ask, with unsubstantiated hope, where did he go?

We had one more visitor during the next three and a half years, Pepe's friend Mario from Gibraltar. I was very ambivalent about meeting Mario, delighted for Pepe for I knew he had a great affection for his old friend but wary on my own behalf as, on hearing of our intention to marry, Mario had written to Pepe. Not a letter of congratulation, wishing us well, but advising against it as he felt that I – or marriage – would stifle Pepe's creativity. I was determined I would never do that and hope to this day and it hasn't proved true, and felt sore at the assumption being made without Mario having met me. In subsequent years, having revised his opinion, he has become a good, loving friend to us both. Recently we visited Gibraltar – for Pepe his first return to his homeland in close on fifty years – and we talked over old times. It all seems a very long time ago now.

Our time in Wales was coming to an end. On graduating in 1966 Pepe had applied for teaching posts, initially in Wales as we would have liked to stay, but then, when nothing was available, further afield. He accepted a teaching post in Grays, in Essex and went a month ahead of us to find accommodation. We followed in September, a few days before he started teaching at the local Boys' Secondary School, later to become a large mixed Comprehensive. I, with six small children, the youngest, Virginia, just three weeks old, travelled the ten-hour journey in the back of the removal van. The removal men, after they had recovered from the shock of being told we would be travelling with them, as we had no money left for train fares, were wonderful. After stacking our worldly goods in first they set out the back of the van comfortably with our sofa, the pram, a packing-case for a table, the essential potty, reading and colouring books and packets of sandwiches, nappies, bottles of milk and lots of water. They were worried about the possibility of fumes (I hadn't thought of that) and made frequent stops so that the children could get out and picnic on grass verges. They thought it was a great adventure and we arrived at the Council house Pepe had obtained for us tired but unscathed.

Ahead of us lay nineteen years in Grays. Pepe, always hard-working and conscientious, created a very successful Art Department which included Photography and Film-making and got his school into the Guinness Book of Records. The end of the first year brought us the last of our so-wanted large family, Sophie.

I have some lovely, vivid memories of those early time: the children on the climbing frame in the back garden or riding the Mobo rocking horse; taking them with me, little ones in the pram, to fields on a nearby farm to spend the day pea-picking; attending their first music and dancing classes, the fun of bath time, two or three in together, Pepe lifting them out one by one squealing their protests, wrapping them in a huge bath towel to dry them, followed by the ritual of bedtime stories. I see the older ones, wellie-booted, going off with their Dad for walks in the Quarry. I remember us getting them all up from bed one hot summer's night when we had all been awakened by a storm and letting them run out, naked, in the rain so that they wouldn't be afraid of storms as I had been as a child. And I remember, too, another midnight adventure when we got them up to see the fluorescent green plankton on the sea at Jaywick Sands where we spent one of our few holidays.

In my mind's eye I have images of lines of nappies, boiled white in a bucket on the gas stove, blowing in the breeze, the picture of my little ones sitting, spellbound, in front of our first automatic washing machine, their eyes fixed on the glass window following the movement, the kitchen echoing with their shrill screams of delight when they spotted something of their own. 'Them's my knickers!', 'Look – my socks!' I don't think anything, even the acquisition of our first television some time later, produced quite the same excitement. I see me sorting through the washing trying to pair up the girls' white socks. Why did they come out of the washing machine all different lengths and shades of whiteness? I would start with a carrier-bag full, match up those that were close then discard the odd ones. A few more washes and what was I left with? Another bag of odd socks. One of life's unsolvable mysteries. My idea of Hell in those days was of an eternity pairing up odd socks. This image of me must be stuck somewhere in the children's minds too, for Jonathan referred to it in something he wrote, aged almost seven. The piece was in two parts, one to Mummy, the other to Daddy. On each had had written a list of what he appreciated about us. I suspect this may have been stimulated by questions in school. On his Dad's list were *you earn money for us; you play football with me; you got us a new house.* On mine, among the expected household tasks, one stood out. *You do the paring socks!*

Was it really as I am remembering it? Or has the beam of light resting upon it through the distance of years given it a gleam it didn't have? I don't think so, for I remember well the powerful, almost overwhelming, feelings of love I had for them and, despite the problems and heartaches caused by Pepe's bouts of depression, I was content. Later, with the onset of Jonathan's illness, we lived through darker times but still we kept that core of love and hope. The hope for our son was lost with him, but the love remains.

These years in Grays saw the forging of more good, strong friendships. We had lovely next-door neighbours, Lahki and David Shiner and their children who made us all so welcome. There was a group of us, Pierina, Madeleine, Sheilagh, Clare, all young mothers, who discussed, with great pride, our inimitable children. We shared a lot of our problems and, after a session in the coffee shop in Town or in each other's houses, would usually return home feeling a lot better. There was Vera, the children's piano teacher, who became a dear friend and who gave me unstinting help with putting tadpoles on wall-bars when I, with no musical knowledge whatsoever, was writing songs for my Children's Theatre performances. I would write the lyrics, 'la-la-la' the tune in my head and she would note it down. Friendship indeed. And there were the Suttons who gave me invaluable help with costumes and sets. I had started the Children's Theatre Workshop soon after our arrival in Grays and this continued until our retirement to Cornwall in 1985 – where I started up again. I missed working and I missed the children.

When Sophie had turned three, I returned to Nursing at South Ockendon Hospital, on night duty to allow time for my growing family and the Workshop. Although Pepe's salary and his evening classes supplied sufficient for our needs I felt I needed to contribute to the family purse to help facilitate the children's interests and pleasures. More memorable and continuing friendships, particularly with Richard and Betty Jones who, having no children at that time were wonderful to mine and were, on duty, the best people I have every worked with. I also became very close to the Yeoh family who took my little ones to their hearts as I have done theirs some years later. After I finished at the hospital I spent a couple of years travelling up to London daily to teach at the Barbara Speake Stage School, where Virginia, then aged nine, had been offered a place after being seen in 'Dream Whispers', one of my Workshop shows. We didn't want Virginia to board in London but neither did we want her to miss the opportunity she had been offered, so accepting the post to work in the School and travel with her seemed a good option. It was due to travelling by train every day that we made more special friends, Steve and Peggy Davies, with whom we are still in contact. Working at Speake's was an interesting and pleasant experience but, as soon as Virginia could travel alone, I left to find part-time work nearer home. Although my family was growing-up now and had less need of me I felt, with the travelling time as well, I was spending too little time with the others. They probably didn't mind too much, they were busy doing their own thing and probably not wanting Mum to involve too much, but I missed them and the hubbub of family life. A full-time job had not been such a good idea after all. I still had the Workshop on Saturdays, which I extended into a couple of evenings a week, and started to work in a local school for children with learning difficulties and to contribute articles to a local newspaper. I decided to do the Youth Service Training Course which led to an appointment as Assistant Warden in a local Youth Club and to my contact with Israel, a land I have returned to many times and have learned to love. Israel has given me more wonderful friends: My dear Miri; Hava, Shlomo and their children; Betsy; Ialah and Nabil and the Druse community in Daliat, high up on Mount Carmel. Friends who mean it when they say 'my house is your house' and extend that friendship and hospitality to any member of my family.

My life has been so full, so rich, so full of adventure and learning and I have so many more memories, so many stories. Pepe and I, after almost fifty-five years of marriage, are still together, 'like chalk and cheese' on the surface but still with that same core of love and basic values with which we started. We have, neither of us, set much store by material security. I am well aware that, for many reasons, everything we own could disappear overnight. As we see on our televisions almost daily, in many parts of the world, this happens. But for us our security is the power of love, and this, with our family and friends, we have in abundance. My family is my hope, my joy and my treasure and Kahlil Gibran taught me the power and value of friendship when he said 'your friend is your needs answered'. Along with the pleasures of Nature, of art and music and the wonder of books what more can anyone need?

I hope this little collection of memories will give my family a glimpse into what I feel has been a charmed and lucky life. And it's not done yet. There is still more living to be done, more future to welcome, more memories to be made. But by this time the children are, more or less, 'grown and flown' (but thankfully not too far away) so perhaps this is a good place to stop my meanderings down 'Memory Lane'. They know me by now, warts and all, and will no doubt have their own memories. Quite probably very different from mine.

Mum on holiday

Dad

With Uncle Cyril

With Paul on his first birthday

On holiday in Holland

At the Cheese Market, Holland

On holiday in Austria

On holiday in North Wales

With nursing colleague outside Nurses' home

Prize-giving

At our wedding in St. Francis Church, Pottery Lane

Pepe in Fairfield Street, Leicester

On honeymoon in Oxfordshire

On honeymoon in Oxfordshire

Getting acquainted, Oxfordshire

Pepe holding Jonathan. Me with Sarah

Our seven children

With Meg and Oscar in Highview Avenue, Grays, Essex

Printed in Great Britain
by Amazon